AUTHENTIC
WORSHIP

Books by A.W. Tozer

AUTHENTIC
WORSHIP

THE PATH TO
GREATER UNITY
WITH GOD

A.W.
TOZER

COMPILED AND EDITED BY JAMES L. SNYDER

BETHANYHOUSE
a division of Baker Publishing Group
Minneapolis, Minnesota

© 2023 by James L. Snyder

Published by Bethany House Publishers
Minneapolis, Minnesota
www.bethanyhouse.com

Bethany House Publishers is a division of
Baker Publishing Group, Grand Rapids, Michigan

Printed in the United States of America

Library of Congress Cataloging-in-Publication Data
Names: Tozer, A. W. (Aiden Wilson), 1897–1963., author. | Snyder, James L., editor.
Title: Authentic worship : the path to greater unity with God / A. W. Tozer; compiled and edited by James L. Snyder.
Description: Minneapolis, Minnesota : Bethany House Publishers, a division of Baker Publishing Group, [2023]
Identifiers: LCCN 2022047544 | ISBN 9780764240287 (trade paperback) | ISBN 9780764242120 (casebound) | ISBN 9781493440795 (ebook)
Subjects: LCSH: Public worship.
Classification: LCC BV15 .T682 2023 | DDC 264—dc23/eng/20221125
LC record available at https://lccn.loc.gov/2022047544

Cover design by Rob Williams, InsideOut Creative Arts, Inc.

James L. Snyder is represented by The Steve Laube Agency.

Baker Publishing Group publications use paper produced from sustainable forestry practices and post-consumer waste whenever possible.

23 24 25 26 27 28 29   7 6 5 4 3 2 1

Contents

* * * *

Introduction

· · · ·

Anyone who has read an A.W. Tozer book will readily admit that worship was at the center of almost everything he wrote. He might be dealing with a certain subject, but the idea of worship will come in somewhere along the line.

In using the word *authentic*, Tozer emphasizes that not all worship in the Church today is authentic. Much like in the Old Testament when Israel slowly succumbed to many false gods, so the Church today is following suit. Tozer's passion concerning worship was that it always be pleasing to God, as authentic worship, not worship that pleased the carnal Christian or the world.

Once when I was talking to his assistant pastor, Reverend Raymond McAfee, he mentioned that often when he would go into Tozer's study at the church, he would find him lying facedown on the floor in the form of worship. It was part of his persona.

In all his preaching, he regularly touched on the subject of worship. In fact, he preached several series on worship. But everything he preached or wrote about had something to do with his relationship to God, which was clearly expressed in worship.

According to Tozer, how you worship God reveals what kind of Christian you are. In this book, Tozer mentions that everybody worships, even those who don't believe in God. It's not if you worship God, but *how* you worship God that is so important. Also, it is what you are worshiping. In our world today, we are worshiping everything except God. A.W. Tozer's passion was for the Church to get back to the kind of authentic worship that excluded everything else.

Much of what is in this book regarding worship would not have been acceptable to Christians, even in Tozer's day (he died in 1963), as the Church was moving away from what he referred to as "authentic worship." Instead, the Church was bringing the world into the Church to establish priorities, especially surrounding worship.

When it came to worship, Tozer would pick up his Bible and a hymnbook, and he would simply focus on God. (Who has a hymnal close at hand these days?) The significance of hymns for Tozer was in how they focused on the God of the Bible. This was important to him. Today, much of worship music is what Tozer would call a "feel-good kind of religion." Yet worship does not make us *feel good* all the time.

If there's something in my life that is out of tune with the character and nature of God, I cannot be made to feel good. Moreover, if I feel good all the time, something must be wrong. This idea was what Tozer often put forth. But, according to him, sorrow and discouragement can be used by God to bring us to a place of repentance, which can then lead us to pleasure in God.

One of my favorite stories of Tozer is when he was a speaker at a summer camp meeting. He was scheduled to preach in the evening service and did so for the first couple of nights. Then one night he didn't show up. At first they thought he was running late, but when it came time for him to preach, Tozer was nowhere to be found. Someone else had to fill in for him at the last moment.

The next day, somebody was talking with Tozer and asked him very bluntly where he was the night before. With a faraway look in his eyes, Tozer said, "I had a more important appointment." It was later discovered that he was worshiping God all afternoon and evening and had simply lost track of time. That's the kind of worship he emphasized.

In a few of his books, Tozer writes about "Cain Worship" versus "Abel Worship." Cain's worship was to offer to God that which pleased Cain. In contrast to Cain, Abel's worship was to offer to God in obedience that which God desired of him. So the two brothers were far apart when it came to the worship of God.

Many of today's churches tend to focus on Cain Worship rather than on Abel Worship, and yet both believe they are doing what pleases God. Of course, God alone is the judge; it is He who knows the heart and intent of each worshiper.

This book aims to sort out what is meant by authentic worship, which goes hand in hand with our developing an authentic relationship with God, a relationship that pleases Him. We were created to worship God, but after Adam and Eve succumbed to sin, they (and later, we) lost that level of worship. When Jesus Christ died on the cross and rose on the third day, our worship was restored according to the pleasure of God.

And this restoration did not lift us up to the level of Adam, but of Christ.

Tozer said, "If there is anything in me that doesn't worship God, there is nothing in me that worships God to His pleasure." Though this can be hard to put into day-to-day practice, I like the idea here, as it takes a serious believer to worship God in a way He deserves to be worshiped, and in the way we've been called to worship Him. With Adam and Eve, Satan took away the pleasure of worship, but through Jesus Christ it has been restored. The challenge, then, comes with our living up to that magnificent restoration.

Once you finish reading this book, I'm quite sure your worship will never be the same but will have a deeper, more genuine quality to it. So let us vow together before God that, regardless of the cost, we will worship Him and give Him the authentic worship He rightfully deserves.

Rev. James L. Snyder, D.Litt.

1

My Quiet Crusade for Authentic Worship

Many will say to Me in that day, "Lord, Lord, have we not prophesied in Your name, cast out demons in Your name, and done many wonders in Your name?" And then I will declare to them, "I never knew you; depart from Me, you who practice lawlessness!"

Matthew 7:22–23

Since my conversion to Christ, I have had a growing passion for worship. Throughout the years, I have learned more as to what worship is all about and how I can best pursue a life of worship. I hope to continue learning more and more about that. I can't wait to get to heaven, where my worship will be perfect in God's view.

I'm using the term *authentic worship* throughout this book because I want to deal with the subject of what true biblical worship is all about. Worship that God cannot only accept but also take pleasure in. To understand that God takes pleasure in my worship is something I have yet to get over. He delights in my coming into His presence to worship and adore Him.

My crusade aims to address today's Church concerning authentic worship. Too often we allow the world to define what worship is and how we should worship God rather than focusing on what Scripture says about worship.

There are passages in Scripture that talk about the worship that has gone afoul today. The roots of false worship can be seen throughout the Bible and have affected authentic worship even today. Jesus' words in the seventh chapter of Matthew—"I never knew you; depart from Me, you who practice lawlessness!"—reveal the most damaging of experiences for someone. Therefore, I want to avoid ending up in that terrible position. It's not just what I do that matters; my relationship with God affects everything I do.

The trouble of false worship begins with God's rejection of Cain's worship. In the whole of Scripture, we also have Samaritan worship, Baal worship, and pagan worship, to name a few. These have become a problem in the Church today because, for the most part, Christians do not fully understand the biblical aspect of worship. Too often they have allowed the world to define their worship.

All kinds of worship down through the years have infected the Church. Hence I use the word *authentic* because there is much false worship practiced all over the world. Some people believe that if they just worship, they are okay. It doesn't matter so much what they worship or how they worship, so long as they do it in a way that satisfies their souls and eases their consciences. A brief time, then, spent in worship enables them to go back to their normal lives the rest of the week.

My crusade, however, is to stir up authentic Christians by getting them to the point of dissatisfaction regarding their worship. I know that doesn't sound very nice, and what most people want to hear today is positive reinforcement of what they're already doing. "So long as I worship with good intentions, I'm okay," says the modern Church. Yet this mindset carries with it eternal consequences.

The worship I want to focus on here is that worship which pleases God and meets His expectations. I need to know God in the most intimate way possible to accomplish this. It's an ongoing discipline meant to be experienced every day of our lives. In fact, it should be an obsession of the authentic Christian.

Comparing Cain's worship with Abel's worship shows the contrasting difference between the two. Although these two brothers looked a lot alike on the outside—we probably wouldn't have noticed much difference between them—their worship, on the other hand, was completely the opposite of each other.

Cain's worship pleased Cain and the people around him, whereas Abel's worship was not a popular kind of worship. There was blood involved in his worship, but there also was pleasure involved, and God accepted it because it pleased Him.

If through this book I can rouse believers to reevaluate their worship and get on the right spiritual track in this regard, I will have accomplished my purpose. We often want to write something that will please people and make them feel good about themselves. But I'm afraid I will be writing things that will create a little bit of discontent among certain people. Here is my rationale: If I can create some discomfort and dissatisfaction in somebody's heart and life, it could spur them to go forward and discover the truth.

I have learned throughout my life that you can't simply present truth; you must stir up the heart and make that heart hungry for truth. I want your heart to be so hungry for worship that nothing else matters.

When I say I am on a "quiet crusade," I am referring to the fact that this is not a popular subject I'm dealing with, and therefore I cannot shout and so call attention to it. Instead, I must address those things that are apt to bring discomfort to the hearts of people trying to follow God and perhaps get them to evaluate their worship. In this way, I stand pretty much alone.

I understand that this is not going to be popular. I understand that worship today is popular, but not the worship of Abel. Nothing about the worship I'm advocating attracts people like Cain's worship would.

I selected Matthew 7:22–23 for this chapter because of the significance of God knowing me, which is what worship is all about. "Many will say to Me in that day, 'Lord, Lord, have we not prophesied in Your name, cast out demons in Your name, and done many wonders in Your name?' And then I will declare to them, 'I never knew you; depart from Me, you who practice lawlessness!'"

Many people are not doing good in our world today, even those who believe they are in the Christian club. Like Cain, they are doing things that please them. The work they do is what pleases them and lifts them above the people around them. They have risen to a certain level of celebrity.

Along with this, their worship is that which pleases them, and they take pride in it. Whatever doesn't please them is immediately edited from their schedule.

I want to show that my worship is not designed to please me. My worship is not convenient when I present it to the Lord, just like Abel's sacrifice was bloody and not very pleasant. I am not trying to please myself, but please God in my worship. Therefore, I need to bring to God that which pleases Him, and to do that, I need to seek to understand God and His character. And as my understanding of God grows and develops, so then will my worship.

That is the great challenge with authentic worship. Anybody can worship anything, but if the worship doesn't rise to the level of pleasing God, it is not authentic.

What stands out most to me is the phrase, "I never knew you; depart from Me, you who practice lawlessness." So they went through the motions of serving God all their lives, but the bottom line was that God never knew them. How tragic to work your entire life doing things that you think will influence God in your direction, only to find out that He did not accept anything in your worship.

God cannot accept my worship unless it meets His standards, and His standards have nothing to do with my ability or understanding. Rather, I must come to worship God by His terms, and in the way that pleases Him, not me.

Looking at the Old Testament style of worship, we find that God dictated their worship of Him. Of course, through the years, under the Pharisees' leadership, Israel drifted away from the focal point of their worship until the time when Jesus came, and then their worship rejected Him.

If I could use a very simple illustration here, I would use counterfeit money. The danger of counterfeit money is that it looks like the real thing. Most people aren't able to tell whether it's counterfeit or real, and yet the counterfeit money is worth nothing.

Likewise, if we're involved in counterfeit worship, it is worth nothing insofar as God is concerned. The counterfeit may please some people, but it won't please the one or ones who know the difference between the counterfeit and the real or authentic.

Also, true worship has nothing to do with rituals. The apostle Paul said it so well: "There is neither Jew nor Greek, there is neither slave nor free, there is neither male nor female; for you are all one in Christ Jesus" (Galatians 3:28). It is that oneness from which our worship flows.

Nor is true worship a denominational thing, though we tend to make it so. Denominations have so messed up the basic worship of God, that it must grieve God beyond measure. The problem with denominations is that too often they eventually become ruled by Pharisees.

What would happen in our world today if we set aside all denominational concerns among churches and instead adopted the biblical standard for worship and praising God? If that indeed took place, I believe there would be a wonderful move of God among worshipers, and because of that move of God, many would come to Christ. As Paul said, "For you are all one in Christ Jesus."

The authentic worship of God should be the primary focus of my life as a follower of Christ. What it takes for me to get into that position is exactly what I'm willing to do. What I must give up to get into that position I will gladly give up for the glory of God. Authentic worship will cost me everything, but I give testimony that it is well worth the cost.

* * * *

O God, I pray that You will purify my efforts to worship You. May this be the most important thing in my life today. May my worship be so authentic that it flows in every aspect of my life. May I be swept up in Your presence. In Jesus' name, amen.

O WORSHIP THE KING

O worship the King, all-glorious above,
O gratefully sing his power and his love:
our shield and defender, the Ancient of Days,
pavilioned in splendor and girded with praise.

O tell of his might and sing of his grace,
whose robe is the light, whose canopy space.
His chariots of wrath the deep thunderclouds form,
and dark is his path on the wings of the storm.

Robert Grant

2

The Roots of Authentic Worship

Then God said, "Let Us make man in Our image, according to Our likeness; let them have dominion over the fish of the sea, over the birds of the air, and over the cattle, over all the earth and over every creeping thing that creeps on the earth." So God created man in His own image; in the image of God He created him; male and female He created them.

Genesis 1:26–27

To understand authentic worship, we need to understand what is behind our creation. According to the Scriptures, God created man "after our likeness." In other words, there is within each human person a connection with God. That connection, I believe, is worship.

God created everything for a reason, and our reason is that we might worship the Almighty Father, maker of heaven and earth. As you read through the book of Genesis, you find that mankind sinned, lost the glory, fell, and the result was that the light went out of man's heart. Then mankind stopped worshiping God and instead shifted their affections to things below.

All was not lost because God sent His only begotten Son, who was born of the Virgin Mary, suffered under Pontius Pilate, crucified, died and was buried. On the third day He rose from the dead and now sits at the right hand of the throne of the Majesty in the heavens. Christ came so that He might restore us and lift us so much higher, just as Christ is higher than Adam. All we could do as Adam was to be equal to Adam, but in Christ, He raises us until we shall be like Him. Thus redemption is an improvement upon creation.

Everything God does for mankind has something to do with preparing us to worship Him. Or put another way, since God created us to worship Him, everything leads the believer into that position of worship which pleases Him. For although sin has done a terrible thing to us and to all of creation, it wasn't bigger than God, nor did it thwart His plan to prepare us.

What, then, does it mean to worship God? I admit that my definition of worship is an imperfect one, but as I see it, to worship God is *to feel in the heart*. And what does it mean to feel in the heart? This may not occur in prose or with human language necessarily, yet the feeling in the heart, in some appropriate manner, is expressed in a humbling with no pride in worship. It may come in the form of words—through a song, the reading aloud of Scripture, shouts of praise—or it may come by way of an awesome silence.

In some churches I've been in, a person leading the singing is announced, rises to the platform, slaps the pulpit, and begins to talk fast. He's not worshiping God. He belongs on Broadway, not in the pulpit. True worship is to feel in the heart and to express a humbling but delightful sense of admiration and astonished wonder and overwhelming love in the presence of that most ancient of mysteries, that unspeakable Majesty, which has been called by some the *mysterium tremendum*, and which the prophets called "the Lord our God."

God does not redeem us just so we might stop smoking. He doesn't save us just so we might escape hell, though we will escape hell. We shall not perish but have everlasting life. Rather, He redeems us for the purpose of worshiping Him, that we might take our place even on earth, along with the angels in heaven and the beasts and the living creatures, and feel in our hearts and express in our own ways a humbling, delightful sense of admiring awe and astonished wonder and overwhelming love in the presence of that great mystery and unspeakable Majesty, the Ancient of Days.

When called to be followers of Christ, we are not called to give up a few little things and so feel safe. We're called to surrender everything. Christians have been born again so that they might push through, take the blood-sprinkled way, and find the thing after which the hearts and minds of all people have sought and still seek—both the superstitious ones who know little and the learned theologians.

And the primary message of our authentic worship is: He is Lord of all. Saying He's the Lord of *all beings* would be a poor, cheap way to put it. Lord of all beings speaks of a kind of boss over the beings. Oh, He's certainly that, but this wasn't what the man meant when he said, "He is the Lord of all being." The meaning here is that He is the Lord of all concept of being, the Lord of all possibility of being. He's the Lord of all actual existence. *This* is the Lord we're speaking of.

When we worship Him, we encompass all science and all philosophy. Science is great, philosophy is greater, theology is greater still, and worship is greater than all of these. For worship goes back to where science cannot reach, where human thought cannot penetrate, beyond all ideas of theology and back to reality itself.

When Christians get on their knees, they are having a meeting at the summit. There isn't an archangel who can go higher than they can go. There are no cherubs who can make their way higher than they. Christians are worshiping the awesome mystery, the overwhelming Majesty, and the humbling, delightful love. They are worshiping God.

Therefore, I'm going to fall down in worship and say, "How wonderful that I worship the Lord of the sun and stars and of all space and all time and all matter and all motion. He is the Lord of all."

Thus He is the Lord of life: "That which was from the beginning, which we have heard, which we have seen with our eyes, which we have looked upon, and our hands have handled, concerning the Word of life—the life was manifested, and we have seen, and bear witness, and declare to you that eternal life which was with the Father and was manifested to us—that which we have seen and heard we declare to you, that you also may have fellowship with us; and truly our fellowship is with the Father and with His Son Jesus Christ" (1 John 1:1–3).

He is life's soul fountain. There isn't any other life, as He is the very fountain of life, and so all life comes from God and His Son Jesus Christ. When Charles Wesley, in his hymn "Jesus, Lover of My Soul," said, "Thou of life the fountain art; freely let me take of thee," it was as if he were a light on the highest mountain in the land. He had gone past Shakespeare and Homer, all the philosophers and all the wise men, and was worshiping in the presence of the Lord of all life.

Since He is the Lord of all life, He is the enemy of death. He came down and ventured into this cave of darkness where death snarled and snapped its jaws. We called it a cross on a hill, but it was a cave where the snarling Dragon lay. He broke the Dragon's filthy jaw and rose again the third day from the dead, and He threw its teeth in all directions. Therefore, He's the enemy of death—the enemy of my death, and the enemy of yours—because He's the Lord of life. What does that mean to us?

Consider the words of Christian F. Gellert (1757) in the hymn "Jesus Lives, and So Shall I":

> Jesus lives, and so shall I.
> Death! thy sting is gone forever!
> He who deigned for me to die,
> lives, the bands of death to sever.
> He shall raise me from the dust:
> Jesus is my hope and trust.

Because Christian Gellert was evangelistic, he couldn't write his hymn without giving the poor sinner a chance to hear about God's grace and His offer of salvation and friendship.

Jesus lives, and God extends
grace to each returning sinner.
Rebels He receives as friends,
and exalts to highest honor.
God is true as He is just:
Jesus is my hope and trust.

This is what I want to proclaim to the whole world. I want these ideas to get ahold of the hearts and minds of people until a new day dawns within evangelical circles everywhere.

I'd like to be able to make my voice heard to those poor ones in the Church who are living on cheap fiction with the name of Jesus on it, who are living on the smiles and bows of converted celebrities, with the same cheap songs about "Once I smoked, now I don't. Once I drank beer, now I don't." Thank God you don't, brother. It's healthier not to. But if that's your concept of Christianity, you haven't even seen the door of the outer chambers, let alone the holy of holies, the sanctum sanctorum.

So let's make it our aim to push all in. Let's tell the world why He came, why He lived, and died, and lives today. So that those people who were once made to worship Him, who along the way lost their hearts and their tongues and their desire to worship, might be renewed and quickened and made alive and able to worship again.

Jesus lives and He offers to returning sinners a place in His heart. He wants to restring your harp and give you back your organ again so that you can play the anthems and join with the hosts above.

The roots of authentic worship are in our creation. The fall of man destroyed those roots, and Christ came to die on the cross to redeem us and replace our roots back into our worship of God. If I am truly born again, my worship will be whole-heartedly focused on God and His character alone.

* * * *

O God, our heavenly Father, we bless Thee for restoring to us that worship that pleases and blesses Thee. We praise Thee for those roots that refresh us in our worship and knowledge day by day. In Jesus' name I pray, amen.

JESUS, LOVER OF MY SOUL

Jesus, lover of my soul,
let me to thy bosom fly,
while the nearer waters roll,
while the tempest still is high;
hide me, O my Savior, hide,
till the storm of life is past;
safe into the haven guide,
O receive my soul at last!

Other refuge have I none;
hangs my helpless soul on thee;
leave, ah! leave me not alone,
still support and comfort me.
All my trust on thee is stayed,
all my help from thee I bring;
cover my defenseless head
with the shadow of thy wing.

Charles Wesley

3

Our Presence in
Authentic Worship

In the year that King Uzziah died, I saw the Lord sitting on a
throne, high and lifted up, and the train of His robe filled the
temple. Above it stood seraphim; each one had six wings: with
two he covered his face, with two he covered his feet, and with
two he flew. And one cried to another and said:

"Holy, holy, holy is the LORD of hosts; the whole earth is
full of His glory!"

And the posts of the door were shaken by the voice of him
who cried out, and the house was filled with smoke.

Isaiah 6:1–4

My focus in this chapter is on the worship of the seraphim. Notice the worship of these strange six-winged creatures who came to represent what authentic worship is all about.

I don't have any explanation as to why they have six wings. I don't know why they were needed in the first place. There are so many things I don't know, and the older I get, it seems the less I know. However, the older I get, the more certain I am of the things I do know and believe.

For example, I know that there are seraphim. I know there exists another world and it's the world of spirits. This is the world of our God and His Son and the Holy Spirit; it's the world in which Christians are born when they are born again. The kingdom of God is the spiritual realm ruled over by God the King.

These creatures worship God with their presence. They were there. They could have been somewhere else, but they were there worshiping God. So we find them here worshiping, and so we, too, worship God by being where God is. That is the importance of the presence and our being present.

I hear some people say, "I don't go to church. I don't think it's necessary. I don't mingle with the people of God. I worship God under a tree, and I find that just walking among nature on Sunday morning is enough." The seraphim could have said something like that, but they didn't. Instead, they went where there was worship, and they worshiped God with their presence.

Wherever God is, that's where you want to be. And the more the people of God are assembled, there you want to be as well. The sincere Christian worships God with a burning interest in His presence.

Also, the seraphim worshiped God with their service. They didn't serve God at their convenience like many people do today.

They served God freely; they didn't have to do it, for it was their choice. They had three things: their feet, wings, and hands. With these they came to God joyously and said, "Take my feet and let them move with the impulse of thy love. Take my hands. Take my silver and my gold. Take everything."

And so God had everything. If God gets your feet and hands, He has you. Your feet determine where you go, while your hands determine what you do. Because if God can get your feet, you'll not be going to the wrong places. If God can get your hands, you'll not be doing the wrong things.

What does all this have to do with worship? We worship God by where we go and what we do—not only by what we say and pray. Worship is more than prayer and singing. It often contains these two things, but worship is also *living*. Thus we find worship to include praying and singing, doing and living, working and going and serving. We can worship God with our feet by going the right way. We can worship Him with our hands by doing the right thing. And if we happen to have wings, we can worship God with our wings by flying in the right direction.

The seraphim also had voices and testified of their adoration. They said, "Holy, holy, holy is the LORD of hosts; the whole earth is full of His glory!" (Isaiah 6:3). It is my opinion, then, that there's something amiss with the silent Christian. There's a psychological disorder called manic depression where a person goes silent. They will not talk, but instead keep quiet and stay to themselves. Something is off with the mind that causes them not to want to speak. Similarly, God put the mouth out in front of you, and although He didn't mean for it to be opened night and day as some people seem to imagine, He did mean for us to exercise our mouths to express some of the wonders that have been generated in our hearts.

When we come to God in Christ and give ourselves to Him, one of the first things we do is to say, "Abba, Father." I've heard others say that we will be surprised when we get to heaven to find people there who were silent or secret Christians who never talked about their faith or their relationship with God. However, are not the things closest to our hearts that which we talk about the most?

The silent Christian says, "I haven't anything to say. I worship God in my heart." Once again, that's amiss. The seraphim used their voices to proclaim "Holy, holy, holy," and the Bible links faith to such expression. Faith that never gives way to expression is not a biblical faith. For we believe in our hearts and with our lips confess that Jesus Christ is Lord and so we shall be saved.

I often wonder about those who sit around on the edge and have not led in prayer in a church service. Year after year goes by and that person never prays aloud. Perhaps they would say, "I worship God in my heart," and I wonder really if they do. I wonder if they are simply excusing the fact that they haven't taken in enough spiritual meat to get their mouths working, opening them in prayer and worship. God gave the seraphim voices. I don't know what they sounded like. Being seraphim, I would suppose they had musical voices. Regardless, they were talking and expressing themselves in their adoration of God.

Now the question is, has God got your voice? And can God look to you to testify, to bear witness? Is there something in you, like an impulse, that wants to talk about Him and His greatness? Or do you discreetly keep your mouth shut and say nothing? You know all about the world's ways, but has God got your voice when it comes to God in Christ? And can you talk to your schoolmates and friends about the Lord Jesus? Can you say a word about Him? Do you dare bow your head in a moment of silence and thanksgiving before you eat? Does your voice belong to God?

Notice how the seraphim's voices were both modest and reverent, for they covered their feet and their faces. I suppose the main reason for covering their faces was because of the presence of the holy God. Reverence is a beautiful thing and yet it's so rare these days. Some churches try to superinduce reverence by putting up statues and having windows with the light filtering through or by installing carpet on the floor. More often than not, such superficial efforts only serve to make you feel as if you're at a funeral.

So the seraphim reverently covered their faces before the Almighty God because here was the great God. Their worship was pure and spontaneous, it was voluntary, and it was *fire*. That word means a fiery burner. How much fire do you have inside of you? These wondrous creatures inhabit that other world, worshiping God day and night in His temple, and they were called *burners*.

I sometimes wonder about the fervency of our spiritual desire. How fervent are we really? Jesus said to the Church, "You have left your first love" (Revelation 2:4). He's not speaking of first love as the first time, but as first in degree. If we don't love God with the fervency that we used to love Him, this grieves God and indicates the backsliding of the individual's heart. These burners are before us as examples. God called them to look heavenward, and they've served day and night with the same fervency of spirit. How about your heart?

Are you a fervent Christian? Are you warmhearted to the point of heat? Is there fire inside your spirit?

Perhaps you're religious and you know you're converted, but are you filled with fire? He shall baptize you with the Holy Ghost and fire. Some say that means judgment, and they've twisted the meaning here, but He came by fire when the Holy Ghost came. When He entered and set upon them, tons of iron sat upon their foreheads, and they went out to be men and women of fire. The fire we need in the Church today is an inward fervency that boils. I believe God wants to keep the spirit clear all the way through, until suddenly we are awakened to the fact that heaven and earth are full of the glory of God.

The English poet Thomas Traherne said it so well: "Your enjoyment of the world is never right, till every morning you awake in Heaven: see yourself in your Father's palace and look upon the skies, the earth, and the air as celestial joys: having such a reverend esteem of all, as if you were among the angels."

We ought not to be satisfied with being mere born-again Christians. We've ridden that term until it's almost offensive to hear it. "I'm born again, I'm born again." Okay, I know you're born again, and thank God for that. If you weren't, you'd never see the kingdom of heaven. But a one-day-old baby might as well pose for fifty years that it had been. The business of the day-old baby is to grow and develop. The business of the born-again Christian is to enter into the holiness of the Holy Ghost, to surrender one's hands and feet, voice and mind and presence all to the Lord Jesus Christ and so be filled with the fire of His love.

Another hymn writer, John Bowring, put it this way:

> Almighty One! I bend in dust before thee;
> Even so veiled cherubs bend;
> In calm and still devotion I adore thee,
> All-wise, all-present Friend!
> Thou to the earth its emerald robes hast given,
> Or curtained it in snow;
> And the bright sun, and the soft moon in heaven,
> Before thy presence bow.

The trouble in the Church today is the absence of this spiritual ecstasy Bowring wrote about in his hymn. If only Christians could get caught up in such ecstasy. The seraphim were astounding, and every note was a glory.

We claim to be followers of the Lamb and worshipers of the King, but too often our hearts are either cold or lukewarm. Our notes fall flat and are without vibrancy. Let us therefore repent; let us return to our first love as we seek to worship God with our lives, so that the leaping fountain of His love will spring forth within our hearts and from there, flow to the surface and sparkle in the sunshine.

And may God do a mighty work in us so that our spiritual fervency and the authenticity of our worship become manifest in our presence before Him.

* * * *

O God, I long to be in Thy presence and adore Thee for who and what Thou art. May my passion for Thee constantly bring me into Thy presence in a way that pleases Thee. In Jesus' name, amen.

HOLY, HOLY, HOLY! LORD GOD ALMIGHTY!

Holy, holy, holy! Lord God Almighty!
Early in the morning our song shall rise to thee.
Holy, holy, holy, merciful and mighty!
God in three persons, blessed Trinity!

Holy, holy, holy! Lord God Almighty!
All thy works shall praise thy name in earth, and sky
and sea.
Holy, holy, holy, merciful and mighty!
God in three persons, blessed Trinity!

Reginald Heber

4

The Power of Praise in Authentic Worship

I will bless the LORD at all times; His praise shall continually be in my mouth. My soul shall make its boast in the LORD; the humble shall hear of it and be glad. Oh, magnify the LORD with me, and let us exalt His name together.

Psalm 34:1–3

I t would be rather difficult to present a new truth about praise because it's well known to all theologians that true religion lies in the will. The Bible declares as much. What the heart wills to be, the character will become. And what the heart determines, God accepts as real. The soul swims in line with whatever the heart determines. "I will," says the man of God.

We have the impression that David ran about with a harp in his hand continually and never ceased to praise God. It's worth noting that David used the word *will* a great deal. He determined some things, made his vows, and stuck to them. He knew that what he was determined to be, without a doubt God would see that he became this. If the heart determines, your will is set and your emotions will follow. So, the man of God said what he willed to do, and what he was determined to do was to bless the Lord.

One of the most misused words in the English language is the word *blessed*. We ask the Lord to bless us when we don't know what else to say. I do it myself. It's one of those big, stretching tarpaulin words that tends to cover everything. Though the word could be used to mean almost anything, here it means to salute, congratulate, or praise. Therefore, he said, "I will salute the Lord at all times, and I will congratulate God."

Let me break this down a bit by suggesting what it means for a man to get up in the morning, congratulate the Almighty God on who He is and what He has been doing and what He is doing and what He plans to do, offer God earnest and sincere congratulations, and praise and please God. All of these can be found in the word *blessed*, spoken in Hebrew by the man David. In essence he said, "I will salute God, and I will congratulate Him. And I will make this my business in life to offer congratulations to the Lord God Almighty because of His greatness."

It's amusing to see how greatness is relative. Greatness is either big or little, depending on what we're comparing it to. But when it comes to the Almighty God, all the bars are down, and all the limits are off. The greatness of God exceeds all wards, cities, states, countries, empires, worlds, and universes. God is greater than all greatness and mightier than all might.

So we salute and congratulate God because of His greatness and holiness.

Against the background of such unholy carryings-on as human beings are capable of, thinking of God's holiness is a healing and consoling thing. I determined that I will congratulate God because He's holy. He is holy beyond all holiness. Holier than the angels. Holier than the seraphim who burn at the throne. Holier than the holiest man or woman who ever lived. He is a holy God, infinitely and perfectly holy. Every day I'm going to salute God because of His holiness, and then, because of His kindness and providence and atonement and mercy and care, His praise shall continually be in my mouth.

We have words in our mouths continually—profane or unclean words, complaining words, gossiping words, boasting words, empty words, mundane words, or other words. Our mouths are always full of words. When I think of the beauty and versatility of the English language—capable of almost infinite variations, subtleties, overtones, and undertones—and the coarse, grotesque way some people choose to use it, I liken this to hearing a symphony orchestra play "Pop Goes the Weasel." Or worse, like using a priceless Stradivarius violin to pound nails into a chicken coop. If you don't have the praise of God in your mouth, you're likely to have some other words, including a vocabulary that might be considered profane or unclean.

There are complaining words. If the praise of God is not in your mouth, chances are you will find complaining words in your mouth. Of course, instead of complaining, we should continually have His praise in our mouths. "But," you say, "there's a lot around us to complain about," and I don't doubt that. While it's true there is much to complain about in the world, if we complain about everything there is to complain about, we're not likely to get much else done.

There are gossiping words. If all the gossiping words expressed across the North American continent this coming week were suddenly outlawed, there would be a silence such as has not been heard for a long time between the Atlantic and the Pacific. Gossip is nonetheless practiced day in, day out, and it's practiced even by Christians.

There are boasting words. Most of us tend to want to talk about ourselves. Some boast very tenderly and gingerly. I've even heard preachers boast and then add, "I say this to the Glory of God," when actually they said it to their own honor, not God's.

There are inane or empty words. Such words are usually trivial, idle talk and lack significance or meaning.

Finally, there are mundane words. Our words are mostly earthly, mundane words belonging to the ground and the dust. If, however, we follow David's example and fill our mouths with the blessings of God, we could keep saluting and congratulating God continually. This would expel all these other words and purify our necessary talk, for as David said, "I will do this at all times."

David was a writer, a singer, and a musician. I suppose it's easy to say that a writer or singer can praise the Lord at all times; that's their business, after all. Yet in addition to being a writer-singer-musician, David was also a family man, a soldier, a king, and the head of a great nation. Much like our own president, David was constantly meeting with the public and giving himself over to listening to the complaints of the people. Through various uprisings and wars, he remained deeply involved, and yet he said, "I will bless the Lord at all times; His praise shall continually be in my mouth. My soul shall make its boast in the LORD . . ." (Psalm 34:1–2). Whether David was singing and playing the harp, or acting in his capacity as a family man, soldier, and king, worship of the Lord was always in his mouth.

God seeks His glory, which I believe is a foundational truth. God seeks His own glory because the universe's health requires that He be glorified, so God actively cooperates in any effort toward that end. And He gives instant assistance to those people who dedicate themselves by vowing to glorify God, to salute and congratulate Him at all times.

Anyone who makes such a vow is effectively saying, "With God's help, I will put unclean words, complaining words, gossiping words, empty words, and boasting words out of my mouth. Instead, I'll fill my mouth continually with divine congratulations." God will give immediate assistance to such a person and enable that person by the indwelling Spirit to fulfill that vow. Otherwise, of course, we will find the endeavor to be impossible. But with the aid of the Holy Spirit, we'll find it possible.

Does this mean that I must always be going about praising God with a loud voice? No, it doesn't mean that. It does mean that my determination to praise God is a commitment to form a habit. A habit of praising Him regardless of our circumstances, audibly under the right conditions, and silently when speech would be unseemly. I suppose this is why God's people often come across poorly with the public, because we're zealots in the kingdom of God—and we all ought to be zealots, fanatical and uncompromising in pursuit of our religious ideals. One who is zealous can never compromise, which is what we need in today's compromising Church. Yet some in the kingdom of God are so filled with zeal that they don't seem to understand when to speak and when to keep quiet.

Spirit-led Christians make blessing God a constant habit of their lives, and then when the conditions are right, they audibly praise the Lord. And when conditions are not right, when speech would be unseemly, they then praise the Lord silently.

I'm having to break myself of the habit of silent prayer because I've come to pray silently so much that I feel I must correct this tendency by praying aloud more often. Thus we can learn both silent and audible prayer and so bless God determinedly, offering salutations and congratulations to the Almighty God for who He is. Because it's proper that we should fill our hearts and mouths with His praises at all times.

This is one of the mighty trifles that will transform our lives if only we let it. Now, there are things inside your mortal body so trifling that they wouldn't get the attention of anyone, yet they're there just the same. And if these trifles disappeared from your body for even a day, you would begin to get sick; after a week without them, you would likely die. They're called *vitamins*, and they are not good in themselves except that they act as catalysts to set off certain other reactions inside your body, all of which is necessary for the sustaining of your life.

This little thing that I'm giving you is a trifle. Probably nobody will write a book about it, nobody would preach a series of sermons on it, and it will never get into the newspaper. Nobody will quote a pastor who says, "Praise will drive out gloom." Nobody is interested in anything like that. It's a mighty trifle, so small that we're likely to overlook it, but so big that it will change the direction of our lives. If we let our minds and hearts and mouths be filled with words that are unclean, complaining, gossiping, boasting, empty, or earthly, we will go in that direction. But if we insist upon filling our mouths with congratulations to the Lord God Almighty under all circumstances and learn the joy of inward prayer and of sending up incense from our hearts continually to God, again, it will change the whole direction of our lives.

This is the importance of our hymnal. I believe that if we were to take a hymn, memorize it, and hum it when we're in the worst possible mental state when our moods are down and we don't feel like praising God—God would honor our determination and give us the ability and create in us the habit of always praising Him, saluting and congratulating the great Almighty God, for this is what we'll be doing when we get to heaven someday. Never will anybody complain in heaven, so if you are doing a lot of complaining, remember it's going to be cut off very suddenly on the day you enter heaven. It's better, then, that we get used to praising God now, so that our souls are indeed prepared for that day.

We ought to keep our hearts in tune all the time. If our hearts' true desire is to praise God, no matter our ability to feel like doing so, God will accept it. Praise Him always, therefore, whether you feel like it or not. May His praise continually be in our mouths. "Oh, magnify the Lord with me, and let us exalt His name together" (Psalm 34:3).

Praising God has the power to usher us into that realm of authentic worship that pleases Him. And worshiping Him should be an ongoing and developing discipline in the spiritual life of each Christian.

* * * *

*Our heavenly Father, we salute You, congratulate You,
and offer You praise from our well-tuned hearts. May
we never run out of praise of You. In Jesus' name, amen.*

AWAKE, MY SOUL, IN JOYFUL LAYS

Awake, my soul, in joyful lays,
And sing thy great Redeemer's praise;
He justly claims a song for me,
His loving-kindness, oh, how free!

Then let me mount and soar away
To the bright world of endless day;
And sing with raptures and surprise,
His loving-kindness in the skies.

Samuel Medley

5

God's Holiness in Authentic Worship

All the angels stood around the throne and the elders and the four living creatures, and fell on their faces before the throne and worshiped God, saying:

"Amen! Blessing and glory and wisdom, thanksgiving and honor and power and might, be to our God forever and ever. Amen."

Then one of the elders answered, saying to me, "Who are these arrayed in white robes, and where did they come from?"

And I said to him, "Sir, you know."

So he said to me, "These are the ones who come out of the great tribulation, and washed their robes and made them white in the blood of the Lamb. Therefore they are before the throne of God, and serve Him day and night in His temple. And He who sits on the throne will dwell among them. . . ."

Revelation 7:11–15

We see that the presence of this Holy One only allows holy beings. Yet in our humanistic day of watered-down and sentimental Christianity, which loudly blows its nose and makes God into a poor, weak old man, that sense of the holy isn't upon the Church. There is an unapproachable, indescribable quality that's inherent in the awesome holiness of God, but it seems we have lost the sense of this, and of the Holy One, in our gatherings almost altogether.

There are people in the presence of God by technical redemption only. Technical redemption is simply saying the right thing and going through the right motions. If I do that, I'm a Christian. What I worry about in this hour is that we are technical Christians, and we can prove that we're Christians. Anyone can open a Greek lexicon and show you that you are a saint. But I am afraid of that kind of Christianity, because if I haven't felt the sense of vileness by contrast with that sense of unapproachable and indescribable holiness, I wonder if I have ever been hit hard enough to really repent. And if I don't repent, I wonder if I can believe. We're told, "Just believe it, brother, just believe it! Now, let me take your name and address; what church would you like to go to?" We have it all fixed up, but I am afraid our forefathers knew God differently. Religious formulas do not work.

Bishop Usher (1581–1656) used to go down by the riverbank, kneel by a log, and repent of his sins all Saturday afternoon. He felt how incurably vile he was. He couldn't stand the dingy gray which was the whitest thing he had compared to the unapproachable shining whiteness of God. His passion for holiness completely drove his life.

In Ezekiel 1:10, we see creatures coming out of a fire. God speaks of himself often as fire: "For our God is a consuming fire" (Hebrews 12:29); and "Who among us shall dwell with the devouring fire? Who among us shall dwell with everlasting burnings?" (Isaiah 33:14).

This is sometimes used as a text to address the question, "Who is it that's going to hell?" Yet if you read the verse above in context, this does not describe hell at all. And if you go to almost any of the commentators, they say this is not hell because the following passage says, "Who may stand in His holy place? He who has clean hands and a pure heart, who has not lifted up his soul to an idol, nor sworn deceitfully" (Psalm 24:3–4). But does this answer the question of the devouring fire and what it is? It is not hell, but the presence of God. "Who among us shall dwell with everlasting burnings?" Do you not know that fire can dwell with fire? You can put iron into the fire, and it can learn to live with the fire by absorbing it and beginning to glow in incandescent brightness in the fire. Likewise we dwell in the fire. These creatures in Ezekiel came out of the fire with four faces, and they went straight ahead, put down their wings to worship, and ached to do His will at the word of God's command. These are awesome, holy creatures we know so little about but ought to know more.

There God was when He spoke to Moses out of the bush. There God was when He went with them into the pillar of fire. What was God saying? It says in Exodus 13:21–22, "And the Lord went before them by day in a pillar of cloud to lead the way, and by night in a pillar of fire to give them light, so as to go by day and night. He did not take away the pillar of cloud by day or the pillar of fire by night from before the people."

This was God dwelling in the fire. And then, when the tabernacle was made and the cherubim filled with gold overshadowed the mercy seat, what came down between the cherubim's wings? It was the Shekinah, the holy presence of Yahweh. Only one man could approach the presence, and only once a year with a blood sacrifice! Otherwise, he did not dare go inside. I wonder how many high priests ever looked at the Shekinah. That high priest, with all the protection of the atoning blood and the commandment of God, reached for the heavy veil and it took four men to pull away the tapestry. This man who went trembling into the presence—did he dare to look at the fire? Being a Jew and worshiping the great Almighty God, the Holy One of Israel, I wonder if there was ever a high priest who dared to gaze upon that fire.

The seraphim covered their faces. Moses, too, hid his face, for he was afraid to look upon God. John fell down when he saw the Savior and had to be raised up again. Every encounter with God has been that man either collapsed or went blind, like Paul did on the road to Damascus.

What was the light that blinded Paul? Was it the cosmic ray coming down from some exploding body or two colliding galaxies we hear about? No, it was the God of Abraham, Isaac, and Jacob; the God dwelling in the bush, dwelling in the Shekinah between the seraphim's wings. What was it when, on the Day of Pentecost, the disciples were all together in one place and suddenly there came a sound from heaven as the rushing of a mighty wind, and the fire appeared and sat as a tongue of flame on each one of them? What could this mean but that God was branding them on their foreheads with His fiery holiness as if to say, "You're mine now!" The Church was born out of the fire just as the creatures in the first chapter of Ezekiel came out of the fire. We, too, are to be men and women out of the fire, for this is our origin.

Hear these last words that tell us how God shall someday open the sky. The heavens and the earth are reserved under fire. The heavens shall pass away with a great noise, and the elements shall melt with fervent heat, and the heavens being on fire shall be dissolved. What fire is that? Is it the atomic fire, the fire of a hydrogen bomb? Don't allow your spiritual perceptions to be dragged down to think in terms of science. For the awesome fire out of which the seraphim ruled and dwelt between the cherubim and that blazing light that struck Paul on his way to Damascus, that same fire shall dissolve the heavens and the earth. The awesome presence of that holy thing. Don't be bothered that I say "thing" because I know it's a person. He is God, the Holy One of Israel, but there's something about Him that is beyond words and the imagination.

I would recommend that we remember: "You are of purer eyes than to behold evil, and cannot look on wickedness. Why do You look on those who deal treacherously, and hold Your tongue when the wicked devours a person more righteous than he?" (Habakkuk 1:13).

If you harbor evil in your life, in your heart, in your home, in your business, in your memory—unconfessed, unforgiven, and uncleansed—remember that it is only by the infinite patience of God that you have not been consumed. "For our God is a consuming fire," and it is also written that we, "Pursue peace with all people, and holiness, without which no one will see the Lord" (Hebrews 12:14). If you can interpret this verse neatly without being bothered, I wonder if you have ever really contemplated that awesome reality. I wonder if you have the knowledge of the holy. I wonder if that sense of God's over-whelming, crushing holiness has ever dawned on your heart.

It was common long ago when God was the center of human worship, when people came to God and worshiped Him as they knelt at the altar, trembled, wept, and perspired in the agony of conviction.

They expected as much in those days. We don't see the holy presence today so much because the God we preach is not the everlasting, awesome God, the Holy One who is of pure eyes and cannot look upon iniquity. Instead, we use the technical interpretation of justification by faith and the undue righteousness of Christ to water our spirits, to wind our spirituality down until we're what we are. God help us in this evil hour.

We take our tainted souls into the presence of God with a concept of morality learned from books, newspapers, and schools, and we become dirty with everything we have. Dirty is our whitest white. Our churches are dirty, our thoughts dirty. We come to God dirty and do nothing about it. Now, if we came to God dirty, offended, shocked, and awestruck, and knelt and prayed at His presence and at His feet and cried like Isaiah, "I'm undone. I'm a man of unclean lips," I'd say all right to that. But instead we all but skip into His awesome presence.

Somebody dirty comes out with a book titled *7 Steps to Salvation* and offers seven Bible verses that get a person out of their problems and their troubled years. We have more people going to church, more church buildings, more money, but less spirituality and less holiness. We forget that without holiness, no one shall see God.

I want God to be what God is. I want Him to be and remain the Holy One. And I want His heaven to be holy, I want His throne to be holy, and I don't want Him to change or modify

His requirements even if it shuts me out. I want something holy left in the universe.

The problem today is that we allow our churches to stay dingy gray instead of pleading for holy whiteness. As soon as anybody begins to plead that we Christians ought to be holy, someone says, "My brother, don't get excited about this. Don't become a fanatic. Don't you understand that God understands our flesh and knows we're but dust?" He knows we're but dust, but still the Bible tells us, "You are of purer eyes than to behold evil, and cannot look on wickedness."

We hold banquets, tell jokes, and the band plays on, but each person will be called before the Ineffable to appear and on our naked spirits bear the uncreated Being. How are we going to do that? There is a way for us to rise up and offer our sacrifice to God, and that is through His Son and the Holy Spirit, our advocates with God who prepares our naked spirits for the sight of holiness above, where the people of ignorance and night can dwell with the uncreated Being, the eternal light. But don't take this lightly. Conversion used to be a revolutionary, radical, wondrous, and glorious thing, but there's not much of that left. This is because we've forgotten that God is the Holy One of Israel.

Meanwhile, time is flying like a frightened bird. The bird of time is on the wing, and his little wings are aflutter. Soon will come the inevitable when every man and woman must appear to give an account of the deeds done in the body.

I want God to do something new in me by revising my spirit, to change my dingy gray to white. To make me sick of compromise, weary of this checkered living. I pray that I might become holy indeed, by the blood of the Lamb and by the fiery purgation of the Holy Spirit.

Dear Father, we pray that Thou, through Thy Son Jesus Christ, will help us to drive a stake down and say as Israel said when crossing the river, "This is a marker I crossed; something happened here." We pray that this decision may not be a careless one, that we will seek to meet all Your requirements, and that we may in that day rise for the divine abode and dwell with the eternal light because of Your eternal love. In Jesus' name, amen.

ETERNAL LIGHT! ETERNAL LIGHT!

Eternal Light! Eternal Light!
How pure the soul must be,
when, placed within Your searching sight,
it shrinks not, but with calm delight
can face such majesty.

The spirits who surround Your throne
may bear that burning bliss;
but that is surely theirs alone,
since they have never, never known
a fallen world like this.

O how shall I, whose dwelling here
is dark, whose mind is dim,
before the face of God appear
and on my human spirit bear
The uncreated beam?

Thomas Binney

6

God's Perfection in Authentic Worship

Therefore you shall be perfect, just as your Father in heaven is perfect.

Matthew 5:48

U sing the word *perfection* when referring to God is simply stating that He is absolutely complete in every aspect of His being. Therefore, our God lacks nothing when we come to worship Him, and we must keep that in mind. To worship our perfect God, we must do so on His level, which is perfection. This means that when we come to worship Him, we lack nothing.

If God had all the power except for a little bit, and somebody else had a little bit of power that God wasn't able to access, then we couldn't say that this God is an infinite power because he wouldn't be all-powerful or omnipotent. Though he'd be close to it, his falling short, even if just a little, would make him not quite God. He would be short of infinite, and while he would be more powerful than any other being, and perhaps even more powerful than all the beings in the universe lumped together, he still would have a defect and therefore couldn't be God.

For our worship to be authentic, we must come into the presence of the absolute perfect God in every aspect. If there is anything lacking in God, He then ceases to be authentic. And I cannot drag anything of the world into my worship or it ceases to be authentic and is unworthy of God.

But our God *is* perfect. He's perfect in every way, perfect in power and in knowledge. And if God had goodness, but there was one tiny spot in him that was not good, he wouldn't be our God and Father. If God had love, but he didn't have all the love—just ninety-nine and nine-tenths percent of the love—he still wouldn't be God. For God to be God, He must be infinite in all that He is. He must have no bounds and no limits, no stopping place, no point beyond which He cannot go. And yet when we think of God or anything about God, we'll have to think infinitely about God, which is beyond our humanity.

After trying to follow this, some people may get a charley horse in their heads, but it's a good cure for the cheap little God of modern Christianity whom they've been told is the real God. So we pal around with this cheap little God, the man upstairs and the fellow who helps win baseball games for us. That God isn't the God of Abraham, Isaac, and Jacob. He isn't the God who made heaven and earth. He's some other god.

We can create a god just as great as the heathen can. We can make a god out of silver, gold, wood, stone, or by using our imaginations. The God being worshiped in many places is simply a god of the imagination. He's not the true God. He's not the infinite, all-knowing, all-wise, all-loving, and perfect God. He's not that God, but something short of that. Christianity is decaying and in decline because the God of modern Christianity is not the God of the Bible altogether. We fall short of it. I don't mean to say that we do not pray to God. I mean to say that we pray to a god short of what he ought to be. Instead, we must think of God as being the Perfect One.

There's a lot I could say about the divine Godhead and the Trinity, but let me give you a little shock: God takes pleasure in himself and He rejoices in His perfection. The divine Trinity is glad in himself and delights in His works. Remember, God created heaven and earth and all things therein, and man is on the earth. So, while God was busy creating things and creatures, He kept saying, "And God saw it all, and lo it was good." Then God created man in His image. God looked at him and said, "It's very good." God rejoiced in His works. He was glad in what He had done. And when it comes to redemption, it is not heavy work for God. God didn't find himself in a fix and have to rush off somewhere and try to straighten himself out, get right with the angels, and get these foreign policies straightened out with the archangels.

God did what He did joyfully. He made heaven and the earth joyfully. That's why the flowers look up and smile, the birds sing, the sun shines, the sky is blue, and rivers trickle down to the sea. God made the creation, and He loved what He did. He took pleasure in himself and His perfections and the perfection of His work.

The moral necessity of redemption was not a heavy task laid upon God. God wanted to do this. It was no moral necessity for God to save mankind. He didn't have to send His Son Jesus Christ to die for mankind. He sent Him, but at the same time, Jesus said He did it voluntarily. He did it of himself but was willing, and it was the happy willingness of God. A mother doesn't have to get up and feed her baby at two in the morning, and there's no law compelling her to do it. The law would compel her to take some care of the child, but she doesn't have to give her baby all the loving care that she does. Yet she wants to do it, and she likes to do it. I used to do the same for our little children and enjoyed doing it. Parents do what they do for their children simply because they love to do it.

I'll have you know that this eternal, infinite, all-wise, omniscient God, the God of our Fathers, and the God and Father of our Lord Jesus Christ, the God to whom we pray, "Our Father in heaven, hallowed be Your name" (Matthew 6:9), is boundless and cannot be weighed or measured. You can't apply distance or time or space to Him, for He made them all and contains all in His heart. And while He rises above it all, at the same time this God is a friendly, congenial God who delights in himself. The Father delights in the Son: "This is My beloved Son, in whom I am well pleased" (Matthew 3:17). And the Son delights in the Father, saying, "I thank You, Father, Lord of heaven and earth . . ." (Luke 10:21), and certainly the Holy Spirit delights in the Father and the Son.

When it came to the Incarnation, this wasn't something that Jesus Christ did, reverting His strength and saying, "I hate this thing. I wish I could get out of it." Then He came to the womb of the Virgin Mary, and some of the dear old theologians said that He abhorred it. He did not, of course, abhor the Virgin's womb. How could the everlasting, eternal, infinite God whom space cannot contain hate being confined? Wouldn't it be a humiliation? No. The Incarnation of Jesus Christ in mortal flesh was not a heavy thing that Jesus—the second person of the Trinity, the everlasting Son, the eternal Word—had to do. He made himself flesh joyously, so that when the angels sang about the Incarnation, they sang joyously about it.

Notice that when Jesus Christ saves a lamb in Luke 15:5, He carries it on His shoulders. And what's the verb that is used here? *Rejoicing.* He does so rejoicing. He returns home rejoicing. And the same will be with the confirmation in that great day.

For example, look at energy. Think of what you're made of and that everything is comprised of atoms. And atoms are comprised of protons, neutrons, and electrons, which you can't keep still, not even for a second. They dash about in all directions and at tremendous speeds, and the heavenly bodies move the same way. I believe God sang when He created these things. The wonder of all the living creatures, the motion and hurling bodies as they race to-and-fro, the sun and moon and stars working together in concert with the earth—all of this is God rejoicing in His creation.

Have you ever stopped to think what it would be like if there were no light anywhere? What would happen if the Almighty God were suddenly to shut out all the light there is? I myself wouldn't want to be alive to experience it. We need light and color and sound. Some people are afraid of color in their lives. They think spirituality exists in their being drab. Yet God created color and He made all kinds and shades of colors.

Look at the sunset. Is that just something scientific? Ah, you can't fool me. Do you think God made that lovely painting out there, splashing the sky with His beautifully rich colors, and that God wasn't smiling when He did that? Are you telling me that this is just an accident of nature, scientifically explained? If so, perhaps you've got too much learning for your own good. The fact is, God made the sunset. He also made the colors. He made the light, and the light gave us the colors. How do I know? I know because the Holy Spirit inspired the writing of 150 psalms in which the wonders of God's creation are celebrated. And we, too, ought to love God's creation.

If we are going to experience authentic worship, we must experience God's perfection. Nothing less will get us to that point. Worshiping God is much more than just dragging ourselves in from the cesspool of the world and expecting God to accept us as we are. The only way God can accept us is when we repent of our sins and accept His perfection. That can only come through our being born again of the Spirit of God. Anything less than perfection cannot enter God's holy presence.

* * * *

Heavenly Father, we praise Thee that the blood of Jesus Christ our Lord cleanses us to the point where we can come into the awesomeness of Your presence. Thank You in Jesus' name, amen.

CHRIST IN ME

This is my wonderful story,
Christ to my heart has come;

Jesus, the King of Glory,
Finds in my heart a home.

Christ in me, Christ in me,
Christ in me, O wonderful story,
Christ in me, Christ in me,
Christ in me, the hope of glory.

Was there e'er story so moving,
Story of love and pain;
Was there e'er Bridegroom so loving,
Seeking our hearts to gain.

Christ in me, Christ in me,
Christ in me, O wonderful story,
Christ in me, Christ in me,
Christ in me, the hope of glory.

Albert B. Simpson

7

The Art of Song in Authentic Worship

And they sang a new song, saying: "You are worthy to take the scroll, and to open its seals; for You were slain, and have redeemed us to God by Your blood out of every tribe and tongue and people and nation. . . ."

Revelation 5:9

In my state of Pennsylvania, the greedy have gone there and bought out the coal rights in certain sections of the state. The beautiful sun-kissed hills I grew up to love so dearly, sometimes misty blue in the setting of the sun, and the creeks that ran below out to the rivers and down to the sea were all very precious to me.

I traveled back to my old place and found that these money-hungry people had sold the coal rights. They didn't dig a hole and later backfill it after extracting the coal. They took bull-dozers and dragged the fluff off the earth—trees, grass, every-thing—to get down to the coal more easily and lift it out. The result was that thousands of acres that used to be covered with green foliage beneath heaven's blue lay dashed now like one vast grave that hadn't been filled in. And the state of Pennsylvania told them, "You've got to fill it all in or we'll fine you three hundred dollars." So they looked at each other, grinned, and said, "It will cost us several thousand to fill it in, so here is your three hundred dollars," and they left the scene as it was. I went away grief-stricken after seeing my beautiful hills turned to gray, ugly sandpits.

I returned a few years later, and do you know what dear old, busy, enthusiastic, fun-loving, joyous Mother Nature did? I don't know where she got the seed, I don't know where she got anything, but somehow she had begun to draw a green veil over that ugly gash. The land was well on its way toward curing itself and becoming beautiful again. So, despite money-loving people taking bulldozers and steam shovels to gouge great holes in God's lovely creation, the Almighty God put in nature the ability to go right back and, in just a few years' time, pull a curtain of green over the earth and start the trees and plants growing again.

We marvel at nature's talent in doing her work of restoration, but in reality it is an enthusiastic God doing the work. We've got to stop thinking like a scientist or technician and think more like the psalmist or the apostles.

The infinite God was happy with His creation. He was enjoying himself, having a good time in heaven and earth and sea and sky, painting the sky blue and cerise and rose and pink, making the trees to grow, causing the ice to melt out of the rivers, the fish to swim, and the birds to sing and build their nests, lay their eggs and hatch their young. In all of creation there was harmony. It was us, the human race, who upset the harmony of nature.

Somebody is running the universe, and I believe I know who it is. I believe it's the "Eternal Father, strong to save, whose arm does bind the restless wave . . ." (William Whiting, 1860). Yes, it's our Father in heaven, His Son the Lord Jesus Christ, and the Holy Spirit all having a good time in His world. We should therefore never think of God as being heavy-browed and gloomy. When God made heaven and earth, everyone sang together, all of creation in unison, and all the while God shouted for joy.

Now, some textualists may try to put a clammy paw over your happy mouth and say, "The angels didn't sing 'Glory to God in the highest, and on earth peace, goodwill toward men!'" But according to the Greek, they said exactly that. And you can't read Luke 2:14 without getting woozy. Something moves within you. You sense a rhythm. There's music in your heart. For when the angels sang, "Glory to God in the highest, and on earth peace, goodwill toward men!" they were singing about the Incarnation. Later, at the Resurrection, there was more singing. When Christ arose from the dead, though He doesn't tell us in the New Testament, it's foretold in the Old Testament that one of the first things He did was to sing. And one of the last things Christ and His brethren did before the Crucifixion was to sing a hymn together.

I would love to have heard that hymn. And you know how you'll identify it? Have you ever stopped to think about the

Rapture and how some have moved so far from prophecy? They have been scared, intimidated, and chased down the alleys until they don't believe in the coming of the Lord anymore. I still believe Jesus Christ is coming back to the world He made and died for. I believe His feet will stand on that day where they once stood on the Mount of Olives.

I'm not going to presume to know more than Isaiah, Daniel, Jesus, or John of Patmos, but the Rapture is a hard one to comprehend, as it's something that has never happened in all of human history.

You're walking down the street, minding your own business, and out of nowhere you hear the sound of the trumpet and it's louder than anything you've ever heard before. Then you recognize that it is heavenly, that it's the coming of Jesus Christ, the Son of God. And suddenly you're transformed. One minute you're walking down the street, and the next you're somebody else. You look at yourself—no more warts, no more wrinkles. You feel your face, your head and hair. What has happened to you? You've been glorified, and you look up and see the Son of God.

We're going to be singing at the Rapture. "And they sang a new song, saying: 'You are worthy to take the scroll, and to open its seals; for You were slain, and have redeemed us to God by Your blood out of every tribe and tongue and people and nation . . .'" (Revelation 5:9).

The theme of this new song is not *I am*; the theme is *You are*. Notice the difference? "You are, You are, You are, O God, You are." So many of the modern hymns and fundamentalists speak of *I am*. I know we can offer testimony, and this has its place, but we tend to overdo it.

We must remember: Worthy is *the Lamb*. He's the focal point. The infinite Godhead invites us to share in the intimacy of the Trinity. And Christ is the way in. The moon is geared this way toward the earth. It turns, and the earth turns, but they turn in such a way that we see only one side of the moon. And I thought the eternal God is so vast and extends out so far into infinity that I cannot hope to know all there is about God. But God has a manward side. Just as the moon has an earthward side and always keeps its smiling, yellow face turned upward, so God has a manward side that is kept turned toward us. And that side is Jesus Christ. Jesus Christ is God's manward face, His manward side. Jesus is the way God sees us. When God looks down, He always sees us in Jesus Christ.

❀　❀　❀　❀

O God, I lift my voice in song. I worship Thee through singing and praising and loving Thee, for Thou has created me in Thy dear image. In Jesus' name I pray, amen.

O FOR A HEART TO PRAISE MY GOD

O for a heart to praise my God,
a heart from sin set free,
a heart that always feels thy blood
so freely shed for me.

A heart resigned, submissive, meek,
my great Redeemer's throne,
where only Christ is heard to speak,
where Jesus reigns alone.

A humble, lowly, contrite heart,
believing, true, and clean,
which neither life nor death can part
from Christ who dwells within.

A heart in every thought renewed
and full of love divine,
perfect and right and pure and good,
a copy, Lord, of thine.

Thy nature, gracious Lord, impart,
come quickly from above;
write thy new name upon my heart,
thy new, best name of Love.

Charles Wesley

8

The Lord of Glory and Meekness Revealed in Authentic Worship

Gird Your sword upon Your thigh, O Mighty One, with Your glory and Your majesty. And in Your majesty ride prosperously because of truth, humility [or meekness], and righteousness. . . .

Psalm 45:3–4

We were created to worship God; that's why we're born. We failed, losing the glory and the worship. Christ then came to redeem us so that we might worship; that's why we were redeemed. I reminded you of the text where Peter said, "He is Lord of all" (Acts 10:36), and David said, "Because He is your Lord, worship Him" (Psalm 45:11). And then we touched on the Lord of all being and the Lord of all lights. So now I want to focus on the Lord of glory and the Lord of meekness.

The Holy Spirit said through the words of the psalmist, "The LORD reigns; let the earth rejoice; let the multitude of isles be glad! Clouds and darkness surround Him; righteousness and justice are the foundation of His throne" (Psalm 97:1–2). It's wonderful to know that somewhere in the universe, there is something sound and right.

With a bit of good humor, I often repeat something I once heard: "If you are to be peaceful and have peace in your heart, don't inquire too closely into people's lives." The idea here is that you will be shocked if you do. And I suppose a throne does not exist where a rat isn't gnawing somewhere on that throne. Maybe the rat has the crown on his own head. But there's a throne filled with righteousness and justice, where fire goes before Him, and lightning lights the world. The mountains melt like wax at the presence of the Lord of the whole earth. And the heavens declare His righteousness. You can search for a million years beyond and not find anything wrong there; the throne of God stands right. The God who sits on that throne is right; He is the God of righteousness, and all people should see His glory. "For You, LORD, are most high above all the earth. You are exalted far above all gods." That's part of what Psalm 97 says about God.

When man fell in the Garden of Eden, the vision of the glory was lost, and this is what's the matter with us. Speaking of how we had fallen and lost it, the martyr Stephen said in his great sermon, "The God of glory appeared to our father Abraham . . ." (Acts 7:2). The God of glory appeared to Abraham, and God began to reveal the glory that had been in eclipse.

When a thing is in eclipse, it doesn't mean that its light has diminished, nor that its glory has diminished. It means that there is somebody between us, and that shining frame is said to be eclipsed. When the sun is eclipsed, the sun is not one degree cooler than before, nor do its flames flash out from its surface one inch shorter than before. It is still hot and as big, powerful, and free as before it went into eclipse. Because it's not the sun that's eclipsed, it's us. So the eclipse of the sun means the eclipse of us. The sun is all right, and so is the great Almighty God.

We find in the Old Testament that a shadow existed between God and us. God was not in eclipse; the glory of God shone as bright as ever. Then the God of glory began to appear to people, starting with Abraham.

In developing His redemptive purpose, God began to show us what He was. We were in pretty bad shape; read the first chapter of Romans to learn just how bad the world was. We had gotten to where we not only worshiped man, which was bad enough, but we worshiped the beast, which was worse. Not only did we, the human race, worship the beast, but we also worshiped birds and fish and crawling, slithery serpents. And if that wasn't bad enough, we also worshiped bugs and beetles. We worshiped anything that could wiggle or crawl. So they got down on their knees and said, "Lord my God."

That was how much our minds were in eclipse. Then the God of glory began to appear from behind the cloud; God appeared to Abraham and revealed His oneness. That was the number one thing God revealed about himself. Even before revealing His holiness, He first revealed His oneness. It is an insult to the great Almighty God to think that there were two or three God almighties.

Is it possible for two beings to be almighty? No, there cannot be two who are almighty or two who are infinite. Where would the second being come in if one being had all the power? He couldn't have all the power there is.

Then we come to infinitude, which means boundless or limitless in its complete and absolute sense. So how could two beings be absolute? There could be one, but there could never be two. It is metaphysically impossible for two beings to be absolute, infinite, almighty, omnipotent, or any of the other attributes of God. But we didn't know that, so we worshiped everything that moved. And if it didn't move, we got down in front of it and worshiped it anyway. Humanity worshiped everything: the trees, the sun, and the stars, and had gods everywhere, praising them continually.

It may seem strange and almost humorous to us today, but it was a long way from being humorous when God told the people, "Hear, O Israel: The LORD our God, the LORD is one! You shall love the LORD your God with all your heart, with all your soul, and with all your strength" (Deuteronomy 6:4–5). This oneness is what's known as *monotheism*, which means that there is but one God. There's just one God, and we thought there were many. Frederick W. Faber wrote about this in his hymn "The Unity of God."

This was what Christians sang and what they believed, and this is what Jesus taught. Little by little, God came out from behind that eclipse. I like to go back to the book of Exodus if I feel as if I've amounted to something or I get all awestruck by a queen or a president or somebody important: "The LORD said to Moses, 'Behold, I come to you in a thick cloud, that the people may hear when I speak with you, and believe you forever.' So Moses told the words of the people to the LORD. Then the LORD said to Moses, 'Go to the people and consecrate them today and tomorrow, and let them wash their clothes. And let them be ready for the third day.'" A person didn't just go rushing into that awesome presence. You had to get ready and get sanctified. "'For on the third day the LORD will come down upon Mount Sinai in the sight of all the people . . .'" (Exodus 19:9–11).

Think for a moment of the many things God did in the morning. He said in the morning that there was thunder and lightning, a thick cloud upon the mount, and the voice of the trumpet exceeding loud, and all the people in the camp trembled. Mount Sinai was enshrouded with smoke as the Lord descended upon it in fire. And the smoke thereof ascended as the smoke of a furnace, and the whole mount quaked greatly. "And the LORD said to Moses, 'Go down and warn the people, lest they break through to gaze at the LORD, and many of them perish. Also let the priests who come near the LORD consecrate themselves, lest the LORD break out against them'" (Exodus 19:21–22).

God, coming out from behind that cloud, began to reveal other things about himself. He said, "For the LORD your God is God of gods and Lord of lords, the great God, mighty and awesome, who shows no partiality nor takes a bribe" (Deuteronomy 10:17).

We've brought God down until nobody can respect Him anymore. So I'm on a quiet little crusade to bring authentic worship back to the Church, so that we practice accepting God as He deserves to be accepted.

The gospel today has gone down to where it's only good for what you can get out of it. The Lord said, "In this manner, therefore, pray: Our Father in heaven, hallowed be Your name . . ." (Matthew 6:9). And I don't hesitate to say that the Almighty God would rather glorify His name than save a world. God would rather that His name be hallowed before all the myriads, all created intelligence, than sinners should be saved or that a world should be redeemed. It's in the mercy and wisdom of God that He so arranged things that He can redeem the world and magnify His glory.

Our first duty and obligation is to honor God, not to help people. Helping others is something every Christian should endeavor to do, but this cannot be our first duty and obligation. Shoving aside God as our primary focus and purpose is a form of Modernism. "Indeed, let God be true but every man a liar" (Romans 3:4).

Dwell for a minute on what the Bible says about the glorious and fearful name of Yahweh: "Will not His excellence make you afraid, and the dread of Him fall upon you?" (Job 13:11). With God comes a terrible Majesty: "He made darkness His secret place; His canopy around Him was dark waters and thick clouds of the skies" (Psalm 18:11). And "Who is this King of glory? The LORD strong and mighty, the LORD mighty in battle" (Psalm 24:8). Honor and majesty, strength and beauty— throughout the Bible we see God coming out from behind the cloud, or He's bringing us out from behind the cloud to show us how great and glorious He is, reminding us that the glory of the Lord will endure forever.

And here we have the Lord Jesus Christ's appearing, "Which He will manifest in His own time, He who is the blessed and only Potentate, the King of kings and Lord of lords, who alone has immortality, dwelling in unapproachable light, whom no man has seen or can see, to whom be honor and everlasting power" (1 Timothy 6:14–16). Jesus Christ, the Lord of all. And finally: "To God our Savior, who alone is wise, be glory and majesty, dominion and power, both now and forever" (Jude 1:25).

•   •   •   •

Our Father in heaven, how my heart longs to experience Your glory and meekness in my worship. Help me, O God, to realize the significance of worshiping Thee in a way that honors Your character and majesty. I pray this in Jesus' name, amen.

THE UNITY OF GOD

One God. One Majesty.
There is no God but thee.
Unbounded, unextended unity.

Awful in unity,
O God, we worship thee
More simply one, because supremely three.

Dread, unbeginning one.
Single, yet not alone,
Creation hath not set thee on a higher throne.

Unfathomable Sea.
All life is out of thee,
And thy life is thy blissful unity. . . .

Frederick W. Faber

9

The Voice of God in Authentic Worship

The LORD will cause His glorious voice to be heard, and show the descent of His arm, with the indignation of His anger and the flame of a devouring fire, with scattering, tempest, and hailstones.

Isaiah 30:30

It's more important that the Church honors the God of glory than they should even preach the gospel to the heathen. But it is so in the will of God that preaching the gospel to the heathen and getting them saved will, as Paul said, "Bring more people to praise him, so that we glorify God by winning more people." But if you had to choose, honoring God must come first.

If there is anything we must strive toward in the Church, it is that we get back to the God of our fathers of old, to the holy,

holy, holy God of Abraham, Isaac, and Jacob, rather than to the God of our imaginations, the weak God we push around. Instead, we should get back to the great Almighty God.

He is that great God, and if I had to stop, I would stop right there. But I'm glad to tell you also that in Psalm 45, there is not only majesty but also meekness. "And Your majesty rides prosperously because of truth, humility [meekness], and righteousness." Therefore, He meeked himself. *Meek* isn't used as a verb anymore, but it used to be. Today, the word *meek* is used as an adjective-noun and *meekness* a noun. Still, it ought to be a verb. And He *meeked* himself down.

"Let this mind be in you which was also in Christ Jesus, who, being in the form of God, did not consider it robbery to be equal with God, but made Himself of no reputation, taking the form of a bondservant, and coming in the likeness of men" (Philippians 2:5–7). The only person who dares make himself of no reputation is someone who's sure of his reputation. The person who isn't sure of himself must run about defending his reputation. And if he hears anybody saying anything about him that might sully his reputation, he writes a hot letter.

But the Almighty God knew who He was. He knew He was the King of Glory and the Lord of Majesty, and He wasn't afraid to void His reputation to redeem a lost world. So He made himself of no reputation. Now, that's one thing, but it's quite another thing to take on himself the form of a man, a servant. The great God who had created heaven and earth, who existed before the birth of the universe, was made in the likeness of man and became a servant.

After becoming a man, He humbled himself further and was obedient unto death. That was not low enough, so He let himself be subjected to an excruciating death upon a cross. The great Lord God, whose strength and beauty were in His sanctuary, died in the worst form known to the times. He died on a Roman cross, nailed up there to struggle and sweat, His bones pulled out of joint, lips cracked, and eyes glazed. What a wondrous thing that He should be so meek as to die in such a manner.

Nobody has ever trimmed down the Majesty that is the great Almighty God. And when His Son Jesus Christ became a man, He didn't lose anything. The theologian Joseph Barber Lightfoot (1828–1889) said that He veiled His glory but did not void it. The Lord Jesus who walked about in Jerusalem with dust-covered feet and disheveled hair was the same Lord Jesus present with the Father in the first chapter of Genesis.

And during His time walking the earth, Jesus taught us to pray, and the first thing we're to say is, "Our Father in heaven, Hallowed be Your name." If you haven't the time to pray anything else, then pray, "Our Father in heaven, Hallowed be Your name. Your kingdom come."

When the great Almighty God meeked himself downward, why did He do it? "So the King will greatly desire your beauty; because He is your Lord, worship Him" (Psalm 45:11). The beauty in you is not the beauty you have, but the beauty that He could make you and put in you. It was what Shakespeare called the "borrowed majesty." The borrowed majesty that belongs to you, and even the poor tramp who stumbles in the night bleary-eyed, unshaven, and on skid row has buried in him some of the borrowed majesty, for God made us all in His image. That alone doesn't save us, and yet something was there that God called *beauty*.

And so He came down, but He didn't do so because He had to. Never think you can put God in a fix or get Him in a tight spot. God doesn't get himself into tight spots, and He never allows himself to be taken over by others. He cannot be forced into a corner and be made to do something He doesn't want to do.

The great God came down because He desired us and made us in His image. He saw the poor, tattered relics of the family resemblance, and He knew that there was that in us which could respond. He knew that, although fallen and lost and certainly doomed, there was something in us which could respond. We ought to thank God for this each and every day that we live.

Anybody who grumbles and complains and doesn't keep thanking God, I'm sorry for you, and I hope you will repent. For no matter what happens to us, we ought to be able to thank God that there was something in us that could respond to Him. And if God hadn't put it there in the first place, I'm not even sure our responding to Him would be possible. Because if I understand the book of John and the book of Romans correctly, I don't believe there is anything in humankind that can respond except that the Holy Spirit has first moved upon it. I believe, then, in the anticipatory workings of the Spirit.

Jesus said, "No one can come to Me unless the Father who sent Me draws him; and I will raise him up at the last day" (John 6:44). He further said, "But you do not believe, because you are not of My sheep, as I said to you" (John 10:26). Note that He didn't say you're not my sheep because you don't believe. It seems we've turned this around, maybe because we're scared. We're afraid to face up to the sovereign Majesty of the God of our fathers. We've come to think the reason someone is not

God's sheep is simply because the person doesn't believe. Yet Jesus said the reason someone doesn't believe is because the person is not of His sheep. They've not been chosen.

We are an arrogant bunch of self-satisfied sinners. We think when the day arrives that we're good and ready to do what God says, we'll come back home and it'll be God's business to receive us, and He can't help himself. We'd better reject that line of thinking. You can walk away, sin against the Holy Ghost, and be as cold as an icicle from this day onward until you die, and God doesn't owe you one thing. And so the gospel is preached in such a way as to make grace cheap and God cheap.

What does God owe us except damnation? We have sinned. We have veiled the glory of God and taken our place along with the fallen ones of creation, and if we're ever saved from our sinful nature, it will be because Majesty meeked itself down to find us.

When Gideon tore down the altar, the people cried, "Kill Gideon, kill Gideon! He's pulled down the altar of Baal." And Gideon's father, Joash, asked them, "Would you plead for Baal? If Baal's god, why didn't he look after himself? Do you have to run out there and defend him? If Baal is what he claims, let him punish my son. I'm not going to defend him, and I won't defend God" (Judges 6:28–31).

I wouldn't write one line in defense of God. A God I have to defend isn't able to take me across the dark river; He can't save my soul from the magnetic tug of hell. If the God I have to defend cannot deliver me from the Devil's machinations, there is no hope for me, and I'm forever lost. Ah, but my God doesn't need my defense. He's the Lord of glory, mighty and great, and yet He meeked himself down to find me.

We ought to thank God every day in red-faced chagrin that, despite our sin, He meeked himself down to rescue us. He became meek because He is Majesty. And why did He do it? "But I saw no temple in it, for the Lord God Almighty and the Lamb are its temple. The city had no need of the sun or of the moon to shine in it, for the glory of God illuminated it. The Lamb *is* its light" (Revelation 21:22–23).

I have no doubt that many Christians are running around the country believing there will be a brass band a mile long waiting to meet them when they go to heaven. But we see here in the book of Revelation that the sun and moon were not needed, that the glory of God illuminated all of heaven, with the Lamb being its light. As the poet Oliver Wendell Holmes wrote in his hymn, "Before Thy ever-blazing throne, we ask no luster of our own."

"And the nations of those who are saved shall walk in its light, and the kings of the earth bring their glory and honor into it. Its gates shall not be shut at all by day (there shall be no night there). And they shall bring the glory and the honor of the nations into it" (Revelation 21:24–26).

"'I, Jesus, have sent My angel to testify to you these things in the churches. I am the Root and the Offspring of David, the Bright and Morning Star.' And the Spirit and the bride say, 'Come!' And let him who hears say, 'Come!' And let him who thirsts come. Whoever desires, let him take the water of life freely" (Revelation 22:16–17).

Here's the Root and the Offspring of David, the Bright and Morning Star who was and is Majesty, meeking himself down to call us to Him. Though we deserve nothing but death, Jesus in His infinite love suffered and died so that we might be called to Him. Wonderful, wonderful.

David said, "My heart is overflowing with a good theme; I recite my composition concerning the King. . . . You are fairer than the sons of men; grace is poured upon Your lips . . ." (Psalm 45:1–2). What a wonderful, gracious God He is. He's the God of sovereignty before He's the God of grace. If only the Church would restore the teaching of God's sovereignty, sinners would be fully converted, not half converted.

The Lord Jesus said, "When you pray, say: Our Father in heaven, hallowed be Your name. Your kingdom come. Your will be done on earth as it is in heaven" (Luke 11:2). Let these words be first in our hearts, and all the other things will fall into place.

※ ※ ※ ※

I praise Thee, O God, that Thy voice is resonating in my heart. Continue speaking to me, and I will do my best to listen to Thee and to obey Thy voice. In Jesus' name, amen.

THE VOICE OF GOD

The voice of God goes out through all the world:
God's glory speaks across the universe.
The great King's herald cries from star to star:
"With pow'r, with justice, Christ will be the way."

The Lord has said: "Receive my messenger,
My promise to the world, my pledge made flesh,
A lamp to ev'ry nation, light from light:
With pow'r, with justice, Christ will be the way.

"The broken reed he will not trample down,
Nor set his heel upon the dying flame,
He binds the wounds, and health is in his hand:
With pow'r, with justice, Christ will be the way.

"Anointed with the Spirit and with power,
He comes to crown with comfort all the weak,
To show the face of justice to the poor:
With pow'r, with justice, Christ will be the way.

"His touch will bless the eyes that darkness held,
The lame shall run, the halting tongue shall sing,
And pris'ners laugh in light and liberty:
With pow'r, with justice, Christ will be the way."

Luke Connaughton

10

The Secret Place of the Most High in Authentic Worship

He who dwells in the secret place of the Most High shall abide under the shadow of the Almighty.

Psalm 91:1

The word *place* usually refers to a geographical location, but if we extend the meaning of the word, it can also be a moral finding or mental location. Either way, this secret place of the Most High is a real place. It's not a poetic phrase only, nor is it vague or indefinite. In fact, the secret place spoken of in this psalm is so real that we can be in it or be out of it. We can be near to it or far from it. We can be approaching it or going farther away from it. It's a real place and yet it is not a physical place; the secret place of the Most High is not a church.

I don't want you to think you must go to a church to be in the secret place of the Most High. A church building is not the secret place of the Most High. Moses wrote about the Most High's secret place, and anything he wrote about was unlikely to be describing any sort of building. So, the secret place here is not a church building or even a prayer closet.

We sometimes say, "I'm glad I went to church today," or "I'm glad to be able to sit in the heavenly places in Christ Jesus." Oh no, our churches are not the heavenly places in Christ Jesus. Neither can our meetings as Christians be said to be in the heavenly places in Christ Jesus. Being with the Lord Jesus is a spiritual location, not a physical one, however precious our meetings or secret times of prayer in our prayer closets might be. That's not what the psalmist meant when he said, "He who dwells in the secret place of the Most High . . ." It is not a shrine, it's not a meeting, not a country, not a holy land, and it's not a denomination or a doctrine.

The secret place of the Most High is the heart of God, the place of faith in God, love for God, confidence in the love of God in Christ, and obedient trust in the mercy of God. Our state of heart within the heart of God—that is the sacred place of the Most High. We may enter it, we may abide in it, and we may be in it or out of it. More importantly, the secret place of the Most High is there for us.

And it is a secret place not because it's hidden or difficult to find, but because there are so few who enter it. It's an open secret, meaning it is secret because there are so few Christians who ever find or enter the secret place of the Most High. Only a handful of hungry, eager people seek out the secret place of the Most High, find it and enter it.

When I think of how some people, touched by a divine stroke, find their way through with hardly a chance in the wide world—without anything to encourage them, without anybody apparently to help them or even to pray for them—I'm left amazed. For others, however, it remains a secret, and they don't know where it is. They haven't found it and probably never will. It's as unreal to them as the fabled Atlantis, the island supposed to have arisen out of the Atlantic Ocean, staying there a while before sinking back beneath the sea. Beautiful, but only temporary.

So, this secret place is like Atlantis to the average person, and those who dwell in it tend to be different. They're peculiar and a little bit careless of this life. Though they're often lonely, they tend to flock together and know each other without an introduction. My conclusion is that the people of God today are not found in the mobs and the crowds, but are people picked out from the religious hubbub, united together in a bond of spiritual union.

Going back to Psalm 91:1 and the words "Most High." The adjective *most* is clear enough, but the word *high* is used in this psalm as a noun, though typically it's used as an adjective. It's God himself who is the Most High. Often written as the "Most High God," here it's simply the Most High. Both are referring to the Almighty God.

The first occurrence of the term is in the book of Genesis. As far as we know, the first time Abraham used it was when he heard that his brother had been taken captive, and he armed and trained the servants born in his house, 318 in all. He divided himself against the enemy, sent his servants out, smote them, and pursued them unto Hobah. He brought back all the goods, his brother Lot and his goods, as well as the people. The king of Sodom went out, and Melchizedek king of Salem brought forth bread and wine, who was the priest of the Most High God.

And he blessed Abraham and said, "Blessed be Abram of God Most High, possessor of heaven and earth; and blessed be God Most High, who has delivered your enemies into your hand" (Genesis 14:19–20).

Abraham gave Melchizedek a tithe, and the king of Sodom said to Abraham, "Give me the persons, and take the goods for yourself." But Abraham said to the king, "I have raised my hand to the LORD, God Most High, the Possessor of heaven and earth, that I will take nothing, from a thread to a sandal strap, and that I will not take anything that is yours, lest you should say, 'I have made Abram rich . . .'" (Genesis 14:21–23). While there were pagan gods all around Abraham and Melchizedek and the city of Salem, here was the one God over all, the Most High God.

There was also the hierarchy of heaven: the powers, the angels, the seraphim, and those watchers and holy ones Daniel spoke about. But above them all was the Most High God, throned in light, the unbeginning One, immortal and all-powerful. God, the Father of our Lord Jesus Christ, is the Most High.

Again, the secret place, this spiritual location, this home, this abiding place of the heart is secret only because so few know it. Nevertheless, it's in the heart of the Most High God: And they who "dwell in the secret place of the Most High shall abide under the shadow of the Almighty."

There is a friction of moral incompatibility with the world, or more specifically, the incompatibility of the Christian heart with the world. If you don't understand what it is I'm speaking of, you are nowhere near the secret place of the Most High. And if you're familiar with the English words I'm using and yet it sounds as though I'm speaking a strange language and you don't know what I mean, then I would urge you to turn your face toward the secret place and push on at any cost until you enter there, for there's moral incompatibility with the world.

When our Lord Jesus came to apostate Israel, He walked among the people. And everywhere He went, their religion caused an irritation in His holy soul. He was pressed between the upper and lower millstones, ground in the friction of His times. He said, "Because zeal for Your house has eaten me up . . ." (Psalm 69:9). His zeal for God was in the Temple, where money changers and worldlings and hypocrites and liars and rabbis knew not God. When Jesus heard the name of His Father spoken by lips that had never known His Father, this gave rise to friction within the personality of Jesus that hurt and wounded Him.

Only the wounded hearts know the true fellowship with God. The apostle Paul said that he wanted to know the fellowship of Jesus' suffering so that he might know Him. Because of the friction of moral incompatibility with the world, that suffering is necessary.

We need the secret place of the Most High to worship and to find rest for our souls. The secret place is not a place you leave to do battle because it's not a physical location. It is the place from which you reach out to do the battle of the Lord against the foe. Nobody needs to leave this secret place of the Most

High. When I go to preach somewhere, I don't say good-bye to the secret place, like the soldier does in leaving the barracks to go out to get shot at. I take the secret place with me everywhere I go, and we can have the secret place of the Most High right there where the incompatibility is, where the friction is, and where the heat is.

The people of God on the earth will come to know this friction, this heat caused by pressure. Science and civilization have set up unthinkable pressures that create heat. For example, a diamond is essentially carbon. The same can be said of coal burning in a furnace. Yet it is the coal's carbon, when put under tremendous pressure, that creates a heat so high it's indescribable. And that is what makes a diamond.

The pressure, the heat, the competition are all fierce, whether in business or manufacturing or on the playing field. This is true as well in certain areas of the evangelical world, where the competition and pressure can be terrible. Everybody's competing. Personally, I don't care who has a bigger church than mine, and I don't care who is better known than I am. No competition, no jealousy. With my nervous temperament, I would have been dead long ago if I had not rested in God, found the secret place of the Most High, and adopted a blessed *uncaring* attitude toward all religious competition. Let them compete if they want to. Let them boast how many people they have, how many dollars they bring in, and how much of everything they enjoy. That is not my concern.

There is a place where we don't have to live under such pressure, such heat and competition. It's a safe, healing, restful, life-giving place; it's the secret place of the Most High. And it's entered by our faith in Christ Jesus. There you will find not the best people, not the good people, not the people specially fitted for it, but just those who would enter. And the way there is bloodstained.

*   *   *   *

Heavenly Father, I see Thee in everything within my heart. I long for Thee and long to discover that secret place of the Most High, bound with Thee. Lead me day by day to relish that secret place. In Jesus' name I pray, amen.

DEEPER, DEEPER

Deeper, deeper in the love of Jesus
Daily let me go;
Higher, higher in the school of wisdom,
More of grace to know.

Deeper, deeper! blessed Holy Spirit,
Take me deeper still,
Till my life is wholly lost in Jesus,
And His perfect will.

Deeper, deeper! tho' it cost hard trials,
Deeper let me go!
Rooted in the holy love of Jesus,
Let me fruitful grow.

Deeper, higher, ev'ry day in Jesus,
Till all conflicts past,
Finds me conqu'ror, and in His own image
Perfected at last.

Oh, deeper yet, I pray,
And higher ev'ry day,
And wiser, blessed Lord,
In Thy precious, holy word.

Charles Price Jones

11

Spiritual Sight in Authentic Worship

Knowing that He who raised up the Lord Jesus will also raise us up with Jesus, and will present us with you. For all things are for your sakes, that grace, having spread through the many, may cause thanksgiving to abound to the glory of God. Therefore we do not lose heart. Even though our outward man is perishing, yet the inward man is being renewed day by day. For our light affliction, which is but for a moment, is working for us a far more exceeding and eternal weight of glory, while we do not look at the things which are seen, but at the things which are not seen. For the things which are seen are temporary, but the things which are not seen are eternal.

2 Corinthians 4:14–18

It doesn't take a great deal of intelligence to know that the author of Corinthians, a man of God who spoke because the Holy Spirit moved him, is contrasting two different kinds of sight here. First, he was not advising us to try to see the invisible with our naked eye. He said that there are two kinds of seeing, the external eye that sees the visible, and the internal eye that sees the invisible.

The apostle Paul is not telling us not to see the visible, but he is saying that there is another kind of gazing, one that's to be done with the inward eye and not with the external or physical. The world all about us is charged with mystery, lending quality and great value to our lives, but the mysterious parts that can be explained do not explain the value of life.

We can study anatomy and biology and know all about children and babies, but that doesn't explain why people love babies. There isn't any explanation for this. As with almost everything in life, we can try to understand, look at something physically, study it as best we can, yet that doesn't mean what we're seeing can be fully comprehended or explained. What can be explained is the basis and foundation upon which we often rest, but there is a glory in the imponderable, instinctive, unknowable things that have not been learned. They're just there. They give meaning and value to life by which we live out our days in the intangible. The imponderables are the things we can't get at, but we can see with the inward eye.

It's impossible to explain why life is worth living. It either is or it isn't, and most everybody knows that it is. They have felt the thrill of love and experienced a bit of the beauty and glory of God, and they see that it's all worth it. Even so, none of this can be proved. One just knows it to be so.

Imagine a dog running around in the night. The dog will probably take an occasional glance at the starry sky. Dogs have pretty keen eyes. They may rely more on their sense of smell than their vision, but they still have a good eye and see everything clearly. So, the dog sees the moon hanging there, and the stars adorning the sky, but what does he do about it? Nothing at all. Instead, he's out looking for a squirrel, raccoon, or some other animal that he might hunt down or harass.

But David goes out, a dog running alongside him, and he sees the stars and writes, "O LORD my God, You are very great: You are clothed with honor and majesty . . ." (Psalm 104:1). The spiritually inspired poet talks about the stars and the moon, the heavens above, and what they tell us about God forever singing as they shine in the night. Truly the hand that made us is Divine.

Now, both sets of eyes saw the stars in the firmament above, but the eyes of the dog didn't see what it meant. David's eyes, however, were able to see and appreciate the wonder and glory of it all. It's an intangible thing, which is there because we are human, because God made you and I and stamped us with the real image of himself.

The world and the worldly, including religion, turn people's attention from God to earth, from heaven above to this life's veil of suffering and woe. They emphasize the things that can be seen, saying, in effect, "Don't talk to us about invisible things. Talk to us about the things we can see and sink our teeth into. We want to have more: nicer cars and bigger houses, better this and better that. We want to wear fine clothes, get paid more, and work shorter hours. So please don't talk to us about heaven; we want to know about life on earth."

Paul addressed this very thing in 1 Corinthians 2:6–8: "However, we speak wisdom among those who are mature, yet not the wisdom of this age, nor of the rulers of this age, who are coming to nothing. But we speak the wisdom of God in a mystery, the hidden wisdom which God ordained before the ages for our glory, which none of the rulers of this age knew; for had they known, they would not have crucified the Lord of glory."

Then he says, "But as it is written: 'Eye has not seen, nor ear heard, nor have entered into the heart of man the things which God has prepared for those who love Him.' But God has revealed them to us through His Spirit. For the Spirit searches all things, yes, the deep things of God" (1 Corinthians 2:9–10). Here we break away from, *Give us only what we can see, touch, weigh, measure, hear, and feel.* And we rise to the wisdom that says, *The things seen are temporal, whereas the things not seen are eternal.*

The world's woe has been its bondage to visible things, which is true of people in all parts of the world and at all times, not only worldly and religious people but philosophers as well. It's a great error to hold that the things visible are the ultimate reality. They are not the ultimate reality; they are evanescent, passing like a shadow across the meadow on a cloudy day.

The things that are not seen are eternal. Things that are seen are like a ball and chain locked on humanity's ankles, holding us back so we can't fly. Our feeble wings will not lift us because we've got the ball and chain.

The people of God talk about faith and "the evidence of things not seen." I am not asking anybody to embrace a dream world. I don't believe in dream worlds or imaginary worlds. "Now faith is the substance of things hoped for, the evidence of things not seen" (Hebrews 11:1). Faith is not a place where you go and hide or retreat from reality. It's a gateway to reality where we will see the real thing. We're not asking anybody to accept imaginary things. Instead, we're asking them to build their faith upon that which *is*.

Abraham saw a city with a foundation whose builder and maker was God, but Abraham never saw the city with his physical, external eyes. He saw it with his inner eyes. This was not imaginary. God said to him, "Abraham, there's a city. Look quick, for you won't see it long. You're a busy man and you'll only get a glimpse, but there it is." So Abraham looked quickly and saw the city with his inner eyes. He would never actually live in the city; he lived in a tent. After seeing it, he couldn't bear the thought of living in any city but this one.

Instead of ghosts and fairies, we believe in reality while God reveals the real world of substance. It can't be seen with the outward eye, yet it can be experienced with the inward eye.

Christians are given a wisdom that's not of this world. They're able to see, pierce through, and handle things unseen and have learned to distinguish that which has value from that which has no value. They can discern what's real and what isn't real. The world, by contrast, doesn't know shadow from substance. The worldly will sometimes give life to a shadow and then find later that they've missed the substance completely, but Christians know where the substance is. God has given them X-ray eyes; they're able to see through the shadows and so don't waste their time or talents or money or efforts on such shadows.

Christians have therefore found the everlasting reality. I could never let myself rest until I knew that eternity was a real thing, and we will not be around here long to give our time to what we can't keep or take with us.

Suppose somebody said to you, "I have a beautiful house, which I have built, but I'm not going to occupy it. It's a two-story house and has all the trimmings. I'm going to give it to you on the condition that you give up your friends, and you give up prayer, and you give up church, and you give up prayer meetings, and you give up your Bible."

How long can you keep this house? Just five years. Those are the terms. You can have this gorgeous home for five years and then it goes back to the original owner and you're out on the sidewalk. Is there anyone with a soul so dead who would accept such a foolish deal as that? For no matter how costly and beautiful the house is, how well-appointed and charming, if accepting meant that you would have to give up so much and in just five years be kicked out, I doubt whether you would say yes to such an offer.

I'm glad for anything that makes it easier to live in this temporary world, but I lament when that becomes an end in itself.

Jesus Christ our Lord swept all the shadows away and brought life and immortality to light through the gospel. He projected the eternal into the temporal and the everlasting into that which is passing away. He said, "In My Father's house are many mansions; if it were not so, I would have told you. I go to prepare a place for you. And if I go and prepare a place for you, I will come again and receive you to Myself; that where I am, there you may be also" (John 14:2–3). Jesus talked about heaven as a man talks about the house he's bought or the farm he owns. It was real. He said it's spiritual, this spiritual thing that sweeps away the shadows, saying, "'God is Spirit, and those who worship Him must worship in spirit and truth'" (John 4:24). He left us two symbols: the bread and the wine.

The reality of His physical presence is gone. Jesus Christ came to Judaism and was locked for a while in its ways, but then

He swept all this away when He said to the inquiring Pharisees, "'The kingdom of God does not come with observation; nor will they say, 'See here!' or 'See there!' For indeed, the kingdom of God is within you'" (Luke 17:20–21).

He gave communion to us as a man gives a ring to his bride. He didn't give us communion as a substitute for Him, but as a symbol, a mere reminder of Him during the time He's away. A little sign that says, "Now there are two visible symbols, bread and wine. Bread to tell of my broken body, and wine to tell of my shed blood. As often as you meet together—while the world wonders what you're doing and peeks in to see—I will see you eating the bread and drinking the wine, and I will know you're thinking of me."

Jesus said of the bread and wine, "I give you these for now. As often as you do it, do so in remembrance of Me." In itself communion is nothing. What matters is what it stands for, what it symbolizes. It's the ring on the finger of the bride, a reminder that her bridegroom is in glory and waiting for her.

* * * *

Heavenly Father, I approach Thee by faith and I trust You to give me the understanding I need to worship Thee authentically. May my sight be clear, and may my faith be strong as I seek to worship You every day. I ask this in Jesus' name, amen.

ABIDING AND CONFIDING

I have learn'd the wondrous secret
Of abiding in the Lord;

I have found the strength and sweetness
Of confiding in his word;
I have tasted life's pure fountain,
I am trusting in his blood,
I have lost myself in Jesus,
I am sinking into God.

I'm abiding in the Lord,
And confiding in his word,
And I'm hiding, safely hiding,
In the bosom of his love.

I am crucified with Jesus,
And he lives and dwells in me,
I have ceased from all my struggling,
'Tis no longer I, but he;
All my will is yielded to him,
And his Spirit reigns within,
And his precious blood each moment
Keeps me cleans'd and free from sin.

Albert B. Simpson

12

The Manifest Presence of God in Authentic Worship

Again I say to you that if two of you agree on earth concerning anything that they ask, it will be done for them by My Father in heaven. For where two or three are gathered together in My name, I am there in the midst of them.

Matthew 18:19–20

Philip said to Him, "Lord, show us the Father, and it is sufficient for us."

Jesus said to him, "Have I been with you so long, and yet you have not known Me, Philip? He who has seen Me has seen the Father; so how can you say, 'Show us the Father'? Do you not believe that I am in the Father, and the Father in Me? The words that I speak to you I do not speak on My own authority; but the Father who dwells in Me does the works."

John 14:8–10

Since the day Adam and Eve fled to the trees of the garden, there has been an age-old longing to find God. Philip expressed this when he said, "Lord, show us the Father." And this longing seems to be universal—everyone has it. But there is also an inborn fear of God, so that the fallen race of men and women is caught between fascination and fear. I wonder if this fascination has its roots in the biblical doctrine of the divine image—the idea that we are made in the image of God. That which was made in the image of another has a desire to look in on and see that other in whose image it was made. This is the fascination, the longing to find God.

But because we sinned and are sinners, as a result we became afraid of God. Like Adam and Eve who fled and hid among the trees of the garden, we do the same today.

Some, particularly the Greeks, thought of God dwelling in a local habitation. They had their sacred mount, their grove, and rocky peak, and thought of God living there. They came in at times to worship God, who dwells on the mount, in the grove, or on the rocky peak. Then, as they approached the place, the thought that God was there transported them. History tells us of some of their ecstatic songs and dances as they approached the holy place. They brought with them heifers with garlands of flowers around their necks, lowing to the skies, and they sacrificed these heifers reverently in front of the mount or grove or peak. And the poets of the day wrote verses to their deities and sang them, and the people sang along with them. These were some of the efforts of those lost and away from God, who were caught up in the strange fascination God exerts over the minds and hearts of people in their longing to find Him. Yet they could not find God in any of those places.

Then God brought the truth to the world and swept away all errors, fancies, and shadows. He showed clearly what the Old Testament had hinted at, what God had pointed to, and what He, through the Scriptures, had been preparing us for: that God would appear not on a mount or in a grove or on a rocky peak, but that He would appear in the form of a man, and His name shall be called Emmanuel. And He would affirm, "He who has seen Me has seen the Father."

Instead of there being a holy mount where they sacrificed the lowing heifers, and instead of there being a holy grove where the poets composed their hymns to the deities, God now dwelt in a man, and that man was the focal point of manifestation. And as God, that point could be anywhere. "'For where two or three are gathered together in My name, I am there in the midst of them'" (Matthew 18:20).

That God is everywhere is believed by both Jews and Christians, but that there is a focal point of manifestation is especially believed by Christians, and that point of manifestation is Jesus Christ our Lord. And because, as God, that point may be anywhere, those who seek the throne of grace can find that throne in each and every place. Oliver Holder said, "If we live a life of prayer, God is present everywhere."

The practice of the first Christians was very simple. They met in the name of a man they conceived and believed to be the focal point of God's manifest presence. They met in His name, and He was their mount and grove, burning bush, mercy seat, sanctum sanctorum, their holy place. That man was who all the Greeks had been looking for and wanted, and all the Jews had sought after if, happily, they were to find Him. And so when the first Christians met together, they met in His name. And that man, they said, had died to remove the separating wall of sin. That man removed the fear as well but preserved the fascination.

Those early Christians, then, were not afraid of God. They did not bring blood as a sacrifice, for that blood, they said, had already been shed by the man who was also God, and the God who was also man. Therefore, they were no longer afraid of God. But they still had that reverent fascination, which drew them to God as a magnetic attraction. They could not find this God by going to the mount, for He was not there. Nor could they find Him and satisfy their desire for His presence by going into a grove somewhere, for He did not dwell in groves. They could not satisfy themselves by going into a building because Paul plainly taught that God didn't dwell in temples made by men.

Still, they were satisfied that God was indeed among them whenever and wherever they came together in His name. So, the early Christians' holy place or sacred mount was in their gathering together in the name of the Lord.

And, they said, this man was back from death. Though He had died, He was dead no longer, and though He'd been in the grave, He arose and was fully alive. He would be present with them forevermore.

They gathered to Him knowing He was there, not trying to persuade Him to come but knowing He was there. And knowing that all Deity was presently hidden from sight, just as He was once hidden in the pillar of cloud and fire that hovered over Israel, but as Jesus said, all Deity is in Him: "He who has seen Me has seen the Father" (John 14:9). And they were all in one accord in one place. While they were gathered unto Him, their focal point of the manifested Deity, suddenly they were all filled with the Holy Spirit. In the book of Acts, it says, "As they ministered to the Lord and fasted, the Holy Spirit said, 'Now separate to Me Barnabas and Saul for the work to which I have called them'" (Acts 13:2).

Remember that in their gathering together, they had no other purpose. So it is right that Christians meet for the sole purpose of ministering to the Lord, to recognize that here is their holy mount, here is their sacred grove, here their promontory peak rising up against the sky, where the ancient Greeks used to feign that the deities dwelt and looked down.

Their assembling together may have been hidden away somewhere for fear of the Romans or the Jews. It may have been in somebody's house, or it may have been in a synagogue or some other building, but it was not the place that determined God's presence. He could be anywhere. Once there, they ministered to the Lord, fasted and prayed.

In 1 Corinthians, we read that there was trouble in the Corinthian church. They met without recognizing His presence, not discerning the Lord's body. They were not required to believe that the bread and wine were God, but they were required to believe that God was present where Christians met to serve the bread and wine. And because they did not recognize this, and would not, they were in trouble. They met together for other purposes than finding God, at that focal point of the manifestation of the person of His Son. "For he who eats and drinks in an unworthy manner eats and drinks judgment to himself, not discerning the Lord's body" (1 Corinthians 11:29).

The apostle Paul went on to say that the result of this unworthy gathering together was that some of those Christians were weak and sick, with others having died. "For if we would judge ourselves, we would not be judged. But when we are judged, we are chastened by the Lord, that we may not be condemned with the world" (1 Corinthians 11:31–32). Paul, in another place, said that he turned a certain man who was a Christian over to Satan "for the destruction of the flesh, that his spirit may be saved in the day of the Lord Jesus" (1 Corinthians 5:5).

There must be judgment before there can be blessing. I pray that we may be wise enough to escape the sharp edge of that sword; I pray that we may be wise enough to avoid the frightful crushing of those trampling feet; I pray that when the eyes of the flame of fire look into our hearts and question why we're here, that our motives will be found pure and holy.

If a church is to be a real church, it must be a communion and not an institution set up merely to be organized and established. Anyone can start a church, find a pastor, elect a board, organize by getting a group of people together, vote in the constitution, and give the officers certain authority. The offices of authority might be pastors, deacons, elders, and so on. Anybody can thus organize an institution. But unless that institution is also a communion, it is not a New Testament church.

A New Testament church must be a company drawn together with the magnetic fascination of the desire to see God, to feel God, to hear God, to be where God is, like the Greeks in reverence approached their sacred place, or as the Jews in reverence approached their holy place, their sanctorum.

A New Testament church, then, is a company of people who have been drawn together by the age-old and ever new desire to be where God is, to see and hear and feel God appearing in the man Jesus—not in the preacher, not in the deacon or elder, but God appearing in that man who is back from the dead, eternally alive.

This is the burning bush before which we kneel, the mercy seat to which we approach, the presence. And remember that He is literally present, though not physically present. It is a mistake to imagine that He is physically present. Some people approach communion with great awe because they think they're approaching the physical presence of God. But the Bible teaches us not that He's physically present, but that He's literally present. And this is the burning bush, for God was not physically present in the bush. He was not physically present between the wings of the cherubim, nor was He physically present in the clouds and fire. But in all of these God was literally present. So, too, our Lord, the focal point of divine manifestation, is literally present.

And if our coming together is for any unworthy reason, we had better heed the apostle Paul's warning in 1 Corinthians, chapter 11. Instead, let us try to confront the manifest presence by faith, here in the presence of that divine man, who is the point of manifestation. Let us have faith to discern the manifest presence and that this is the body of which He is the head, and this the holy place after the manner of the holy place of the Temple in the Old Testament. And let us forgive each other as God has forgiven us for Christ's sake. Will you look in your own heart and ask yourself, "Am I holding a grudge against anyone?" If the answer is yes, you must forgive. And do not wait for the person to repent; you must forgive regardless of that.

Finally, we must vow our obedience. Before God, we must put away this scattering of our attention. If you could have a baptism of a sense of the presence of the God who holds the universe in His hands, Yahweh, the Ancient of Days and maker of heaven and earth, such a spiritual renewal would change your life from this moment on for as long as you live. It would be like giving a weak, tired, sick man an injection of the elixir of life. It would change you so completely, elevate you, purify you, and deliver you from the carnal flesh to the point where your life would be one radiant fascination from this hour onward. May God grant this to us, this sense of His manifest presence.

* * * *

Lord and Father of Jesus Christ, I pray that I might encounter the manifestation of Your presence, that I might come to the point of not just knowing You exist but also experiencing You in the reality of a spiritual encounter. I pray this in Jesus' name, amen.

WHAT A FRIEND WE HAVE IN JESUS

What a friend we have in Jesus,
all our sins and griefs to bear!
What a privilege to carry
everything to God in prayer!
O what peace we often forfeit,
O what needless pain we bear,

all because we do not carry
everything to God in prayer!

Have we trials and temptations?
Is there trouble anywhere?
We should never be discouraged;
take it to the Lord in prayer!
Can we find a friend so faithful
who will all our sorrows share?
Jesus knows our every weakness;
take it to the Lord in prayer!

Are we weak and heavy laden,
cumbered with a load of care?
Precious Savior, still our refuge—
take it to the Lord in prayer!
Do your friends despise, forsake you?
Take it to the Lord in prayer!
In his arms he'll take and shield you;
you will find a solace there.

Joseph Scriven

13

Our Unity with God in Authentic Worship

Now this is the main point of the things we are saying: We have such a High Priest, who is seated at the right hand of the throne of the Majesty in the heavens. . . .

Hebrews 8:1

We should assume that we have such a High Priest who sits "at the right hand of the throne of the Majesty in the heavens." He is the Minister of the sanctuary, the true tabernacle the Lord erected.

An important aspect of authentic worship is unity. There cannot be worship without unity, and that unity must be on God's side. Everything in this world fights against that unity which produces the worship that pleases God.

This unity is like a magnet that draws us to God and away from everything else. It is what's called *separation from the world* and everything about it. Christ's death on the cross cleansed us and prepared the way for this unity. Some people believe that we can worship God any way that we please. But the worship that pleases us, but does not please God, is not the worship I'm talking about here.

Unity is so essential because my unity with Christ defines who I am. This, of course, is far from what the enemy of our soul wants to happen. He wants to bring all kinds of diversions and divisions into our lives, keeping us from that unity which pleases God. If we look at the Church today, we see all kinds of divisions. I suppose there are reasons for all the denominations established down through the centuries, but in general they have been a great deterrent to Christian unity.

Of course, there are no denominations in heaven, and we need to begin to look at our worship from heaven's point of view. We are so divided today. The thing that brings us together is not so much what we believe, but *whom* we believe. That needs to be the central factor when it comes to worship.

Martin Luther was right in doing what he did because of the spiritual circumstances in his day. Unfortunately, that action started an avalanche of division that continues to this very day.

When I know who I am, this brings my life together, and when my life is brought together, I am now able to worship God in the unity He has designed. When the writer of Hebrews says, "at the right hand of the throne of the Majesty in the heavens," he's referring to that unity which is the basis of our authentic worship. If you read Hebrews 8:1–2 carefully, you will notice there is no division, as a supreme unity brings it all together.

Moreover, our unity with Christ will draw us to other believers. This is so crucial that I can't emphasize it enough. We are drawn to other people who believe what we believe, but that in itself is not the source of authentic worship. We need to rise above our divisions and allow ourselves to be drawn together in unity with all believers.

This unity is not on my terms because Christ came down from the Majesty on high to be the sacrifice for my redemption. Christ came down not only to lift me up but also to lift me away from the devious aspects of the world. Keep in mind—and I know we're prone to forget it—the world is in rebellion against God. This rebellion affects our worshiping together.

Go back to the Old Testament and you will discover the development and growth of Baal worship. This affected Israel's worship of God like nothing else. It came between them and Yahweh, whom they were to worship. I'm afraid Baal has entered the Church today and has come between Christians and their worship of God. The enemy doesn't care how he divides the Church so long as he can divide it.

Is it possible that we have a generation of Christians who do not understand what worship is all about? Can it get any worse than what it is today? After reading the Old Testament, I would have to say, yes, it can get worse, and will worsen, before the Rapture takes place.

But Hebrews 8:1 underlines for us that we have a High Priest in the heavens. In the Old Testament, we see that the high priest was truly committed to leading Israel into proper worship. Through time, that leadership went in a different direction. We must understand, however, that our heavenly High Priest can never be persuaded to be influenced by the culture.

Reading the New Testament, particularly the Gospels, we see that the culture was set against Christ. The religious culture of Jesus' day sent Him to the cross, and that culture is alive and well today.

The notion that God exists and is the sovereign Majesty in the heavens is fundamentally about human morality. And the belief that we are from God gives us a certain upward moral viewpoint that we couldn't possibly have if we didn't believe it. The belief that we must one day return to God and report to Him regarding the deeds done in the body has a strong power to hold the human soul together. So we sing the hymn by Charles Wesley, "A charge to keep, I have a God to glorify; a never-dying soul to save and fit it for the sky." And in the book of Ecclesiastes, it says, "Let us hear the conclusion of the whole matter: Fear God and keep His commandments, for this is man's all. For God will bring every work into judgment, including every secret thing, whether good or evil" (Ecclesiastes 12:13–14).

There is a great deal of difference between those people who are convinced that this is true and those who don't believe it at all. For if we truly believe it, we must cheer for God. If this is our whole duty and understanding—that God will bring every work into judgment, whether good or evil—it will make a difference in us.

Human morality rests upon the belief that there is a Majesty in the heavens. I also believe this leads to fundamental human decency and the knowledge of what is proper or becoming. Human decency depends upon an adequate conception of human nature, so if we believe that there is no God, then we can't possibly have the right view of human nature. Therefore, no adequate view of human nature is possible until I believe that I came from God and that I shall go back to Him again.

So have faith in God; this is the rock on which we build. When we rise in the morning, it ought to be with a resolute strength, a belief in the Creator, God the Father, maker of heaven and earth.

The verse at the beginning of this chapter talks about the Majesty in the heavens, as well as the throne of the Majesty. The Bible teaches the creation of the universe. It teaches that God created all that we see around us, from the farthest star that the most powerful telescope on earth might detect down to the tiniest cell seen through a microscope plus all the other things living in what we call the world. The Bible teaches that this universe is one single vast system embracing matter and spirit and light and mind and space and time and all beings. It teaches us that these are not separated independently of each other, but that they are united and working harmoniously.

If the world had been created where everything was independent of everything else, you would have widespread cancer throughout the vast universe. Rather, God binds everything together, interlocks it all, and makes everything interdependent, not independent.

It has been said that you couldn't move a stone on the seashore without changing the balance of the world. Or that a leaf couldn't fall from a tree without the order of nature changing just a little bit. There isn't a baby born into the world who does not make the world a little different. There isn't a man or woman who dies and goes out of the world who has not changed the face of the world just a little bit, for all things interlock and depend upon one another.

And the Bible further teaches that this universe—and the prefix *uni-* means one or single—this one great interlocking system has a central control. That control is called the throne of God, and all are controlled from that center.

This seems logical to me. Do you know what would happen to the human body if it had no central control? Many fables and stories have been told about bodies that wouldn't obey their heads, so you can imagine what it would be like. There must be a head in every organism or else there could be no harmony, coordination, cooperation, or life. This is logical also because every organization must have a head. If you organize anything, you have to have a head, a president. The president must preside. Even if there are only half a dozen people in the organization, there must be someone who presides, and that goes right on up to the largest empire that ever touched the world, right on up to the world's great nations.

So, an organism must have a head, and if it's true that an organization must also have a head, then is it not logical to believe that somewhere in the vast universe there is a throne where somebody sits who runs it? I believe that. And I believe that one is God, the Majesty in the heavens.

The Bible calls this central control the throne of God. And from that throne, God governs His universe according to an eternal purpose. That eternal purpose embraces all things. Two little words are often used in the Scriptures, *all things*, yet they are bigger than the sky above, bigger than all the worlds, and they're big because they take in all things.

We have, then, the Majesty in the heavens, sitting upon His throne, and we have as well someone sitting at the right hand of the throne. And who is it? It is Jesus Christ, the Minister of the sanctuary that God made, not men, which is why He was there.

●　●　●　●

I praise Thee, O God, for the unity we have in Christ Jesus. I worship Thee with those who also worship Thee and praise Thee for all that You have done on our behalf. Praise the name of the Lord. In Jesus' name, amen.

A MIGHTY FORTRESS IS OUR GOD

A mighty fortress is our God,
a bulwark never failing;
our helper he, amid the flood
of mortal ills prevailing.
For still our ancient foe
does seek to work us woe;
his craft and power are great,
and armed with cruel hate,
on earth is not his equal.

Did we in our own strength confide,
our striving would be losing,
were not the right Man on our side,
the Man of God's own choosing.
You ask who that may be?
Christ Jesus, it is he;
Lord Sabaoth his name,
from age to age the same;
and he must win the battle.

And though this world, with devils filled,
should threaten to undo us,
we will not fear, for God has willed
his truth to triumph through us.
The prince of darkness grim,
we tremble not for him;
his rage we can endure,
for lo! his doom is sure;
one little word shall fell him.

That Word above all earthly powers
no thanks to them abideth;
the Spirit and the gifts are ours
through him who with us sideth.
Let goods and kindred go,
this mortal life also;
the body they may kill:
God's truth abideth still;
his kingdom is forever!

Martin Luther

14

Our Conscious Awareness in Authentic Worship

Where can I go from Your Spirit? Or where can I flee from Your presence? If I ascend into heaven, You are there; if I make my bed in hell, behold, You are there. If I take the wings of the morning, and dwell in the uttermost parts of the sea, even there Your hand shall lead me, and Your right hand shall hold me.

Psalm 139:7–10

There are certain basic truths upon which all truth rests. And if we don't learn and hold to those certain basic truths, then we can't know the others that follow, and we can't know the others unless and only by constant reference to these basic truths. For example, God made us for himself and made us so that we might know Him and that we might live with Him and that we might enjoy Him. But we have been guilty of revolt and have broken with God. The Bible says we're alienated from Him. We were strangers to Him, the human race who ceased to love Him and ceased to trust Him and enjoy His manifest presence.

It isn't enough to live by faith if by faith we mean naked faith without any manifestation on God's part. David was not hesitant to pray that the Lord would show him a token for good. I do not believe that it's any mark of spirituality or any magnification of the doctrine of faith when we bat everybody down and shut them up and insist that they remain quiet without any response from God or proof that anything is going on. Since I'm a personality and God is a personality, there can be personality intercourse between one personality and another personality in love, in faith, and in conversation, to speak and to be answered.

Having faith is more than solemnly, grimly, and coldly living our lives as if to say merely, "I believe," but then never having God give us a response to our faith. I know there are times when we walk by faith, not by sight. We never walk by sight, but we walk by faith sometimes when God has hidden His face for a moment from us out of His goodness. For He said, "'With a little wrath I hid My face from you for a moment; but with everlasting kindness I will have mercy on you,' says the LORD, your Redeemer" (Isaiah 54:8).

So, we must have that conscious presence again and learn to live in that presence. And the difference between revival and every spiritual state that any church might know is the difference between the presence of God and the manifest presence of God.

There is such a thing as God manifesting himself, and God *wants* to manifest himself to His people. How does He do it? Well, He did a work we call *redemption*, which is the work of reconciliation with Him. Many churches talk about how wonderful it is to look up and say hello to our heavenly Father. Yet we must remember this is our Father's world and that all the stars sing about Him, as well as the little flowers in the fields. This is all very good, but the simple fact is that the human race and God are enemies until there has been reconciliation through a sacrifice God is satisfied with.

We don't want to hear this; we want to hear how nice it is to know God. We don't want to know that until we're converted through Jesus Christ, we're outside the walls. We're Gentiles and sinners without hope outside the walls. And these sinful people, they toil and strive, they get married and have children, they sow, they harvest, they build, they tear down, they gather with others like themselves, and they die. That is the human race, and these people are not concerned very much about God and rarely think of Him except when making political speeches or when it's convenient to use God.

The Old Testament tells us how this is the case and gives us a shining illustration of God's redemptive plan. And we read in the ninth chapter of Hebrews that the tabernacle or tent (as it's called in some translations) was a flimsy affair made out of animal hides and wood, and it was portable. It could be taken apart and carried away.

The tabernacle included the lower court, the court of the Gentiles that was not inside the great boxlike structure proper. It was outside and called the Court of Gentiles; that's the people interested in religion. A lot of people are interested in religion, but they're far from God. Maybe they're practicing religion and heathen rites of various kinds. Maybe they're telling the beads while unconsciously moving lips on the bus or airplane. Maybe they're paying respect to religion. When the baby is born or when somebody is married or when somebody dies, at weddings, christenings, and funerals they manage to get to church. There is a rather cynical expression that some people go to church three times in their lives. The first time they throw water on them, the second time they throw rice on them, and the third time they throw dirt on them. These are the Gentiles outside, but they're religious Gentiles. They pay token respect to religion, but they're giving no regard to God's way, the cross, or redemption.

Then there's the inner court, and in the inner court were the altar and the laver. The altar was like a topless furnace with a grate, where the priest could build a fire and where he could lay a beast. He would place the beast on the altar and make the fire underneath. He would stir the pot, and the beast would go up in an ugly smoke. This was the altar where lambs were offered, the beasts, the red heifers, all the creatures that were brought to be sacrificed. This part of the tabernacle was not a pleasant place to be, and the priest's job was not a pleasant job.

The Scriptures tell us that if the blood does not redeem us by an acceptable sacrifice, we will most certainly spend eternity in hell. When we sugarcoat it and take away the slaughterhouse element from it, we've taken away the cross. It must not have been a very pleasant thing to see a man dying on a cross outside Jerusalem on the hill.

After our Lord died, the painters later made His execution appear so beautiful that we could have their pictures hanging in our homes and distribute them at Easter. But it wasn't a beautiful sight at all. Here was a man stripped naked, hanging in the sweltering sun, bleeding from his hands and feet and his forehead down over his face. Here was a man whose beard was plucked in spots by those who tortured him, writhing in agony and groaning in pain. Here was a cross, and a man who had been nailed to that cross. Why was the man on the cross? Because there was only one thing worse than this, and that was hell where we were going.

And so God sent His only begotten Son that He might go to the cross and shut up the gates of hell, so that those who believe in Him should not perish but have everlasting life. So let's not get too nice about all this. There was a slaughterhouse and a slaughter hill where a man died. And a man dying is a terrible thing; a man dies in pain because sin is painful. The man died ostracized and forsaken because sin brings ostracism and forsakenness. God turned His back on that hill while that man died because He will turn his back on every person who doesn't die with Him, every person who does not take advantage of the blood He shed, and so there is that altar and it isn't a very pleasant thing.

The other significant item in the inner court was the laver. The laver was a large brazen vessel or bowl filled with water where everything could be washed. As you entered and moved farther into the tabernacle, you first came to the altar where the lamb had been offered and died. And when you passed the altar, you came to the laver. It was as if God were saying you first must come by the cross and by the blood, by the altar and by the laver, by the lamb who died and by the washing of water by the word. That, then, was the inner court.

Then there was another room, which was closed off by a huge veil. Nobody was allowed to enter there except for the priest. Worshipers could go to where the altar and laver were but no farther. This room and holy place consisted of three important items. The first was the light of the candlesticks, seven of them burning. The second was shewbread, a table with bread on it. And the third was an altar of incense. It's not difficult to work out what all this means. The Church universal agrees that this light was the light of the Holy Spirit, the light that lights every person who comes into the world.

The people said to Jesus, "Give us bread," and He replied, "Your fathers ate bread, yes, but the bread your fathers ate was only temporary. But I have come that you might have bread, and if you eat of it, you shall never die." And they said, "Give us that bread," and He told them, "I am the bread of life" (John 6:35). And then many turned and went away, for they couldn't take that. If there had been a preacher talking like that, they'd have said, "We love our brother, but let's get rid of him. We think that is too strong. Say instead that Jesus is the bread and that I eat of Him; that's what it says in blunt language in both the Old and New Testaments." And the Church has agreed to it, at least nominally down through the centuries. And so we have our communion service, and we eat of the shewbread while the light of the Holy Spirit shines around us.

And what was the altar of incense? Sweet-smelling incense was laid on this altar and burning, and that little room was filled with the sweet-smelling incense that was prayer. Isn't that a beautiful picture? This is what every church ought to be. It ought to be a place lighted by the light of the world, shed forth by the sevenfold Holy Spirit. And not only when we gather at intervals to eat of the bread of life on communion Sunday but every Sunday, with the altar of incense sending up its sweet spirals of fragrant perfume. Sweet to God and pleasant in His eyes because the sight of praying, worshiping people gathered together is pleasing to Him.

Instead, we often grieve the Holy Spirit. The lights have grown dim, the bread has become stale, and the altar of incense has lost its fragrance.

A further explanation might be that this is the Church and the kingdom. The traveler finds the light, the child finds food, and the priest can pray. You are a traveler on your way home, but you have light. For it's a terrible thing to travel at night without having any light.

Without some light, even a little bit, the night can be frightfully dark. Jesus said, "The night is coming when no one can work" (John 9:4), and the New Testament talks about the moral and spiritual state of the world as being out of a dark night. And so travelers desperately need light.

The light of the world is Jesus and therefore all believers in Christ have the light of God. Travelers find the light, the child finds food, and the priest can pray—that's the kind of church, purified and cleansed, that pleases God. When we walk inside such a place, we know we're entering where the light shines, where there's bread to eat, and where there's prayer to be made, which rises to the ear of God with acceptance. That's what the Church is: a company of people committed to this kind of belief, to faith in Him.

Now, there's yet further penetration or I am deliberately stopping short of the inner holy of holies, the sanctum sanctorum. Let me point out that the altar is here, for the Lamb that once was slain didn't stay dead. He rose again, but His sacrifice remains advantageous forever. The cleansing blood is there so that you and I can come into His presence.

The question is, have we done so? Are we doing it daily? I hope that we are, but if there are those who haven't, I point to the cross where He died, and to the blood that cleanses, to the Holy Ghost who is the light, to the living Lamb who offers the bread. And I tell you that you have a right to be a priest of the Most High God and enter into His presence.

*   *   *   *

Dear Lord Jesus, our High Priest, I bow in worship before Thee and praise Thee for the light that Thou hast shown in my life, so that I can recognize Your work in me. May this light continue to shine as I in obedience follow You day by day. In Jesus' name I pray, amen.

BREATHE ON ME, BREATH OF GOD

Breathe on me, Breath of God,
Fill me with life anew,
That I may love what Thou dost love,
And do what Thou wouldst do.

Breathe on me, Breath of God,
Until my heart is pure,
Until with Thee I will one will,
To do and to endure.

Breathe on me, Breath of God,
Till I am wholly Thine,

Until this earthly part of me
Glows with Thy fire divine.

Breathe on me, Breath of God,
So shall I never die,
But live with Thee the perfect life
Of Thine eternity.

Edwin Hatch

15

Our Freedom in Authentic Worship

In the year that King Uzziah died, I saw the Lord sitting on a throne, high and lifted up, and the train of His robe filled the temple. Above it stood seraphim; each one had six wings: with two he covered his face, with two he covered his feet, and with two he flew. And one cried to another and said:

"Holy, holy, holy is the LORD of hosts; the whole earth is full of His glory!"

And the posts of the door were shaken by the voice of him who cried out, and the house was filled with smoke.

Isaiah 6:1–4

O f all the calamities that have ever been visited upon the world, without a doubt the surrender of the human spirit to this world and its ways is the worst of them. I am speaking of the tyranny of things—material things, temporal things, things that are and then cease to be. No monarch ever ruled his cowering subjects with more cruel tyranny than tangible things, both visible and audible, in the way they have ruled humankind.

This is the worst calamity of all, that the soul of someone made in the image of God, coming from another world as a kind of guest—to dwell a while in this world and then to go away—that such a royal visitor should accept this temporal place as if it were their final home and settle down to it, judge themselves by it, adopt its ways, collaborate with fellow inhabitants, and give themselves up to the enjoyment of a world that is passing away.

There has never been any woe as bad as this, that we who are made for many worlds should accept this one world as our ultimate home. That we who are meant to commune with angels and archangels and seraphim—and of course firstly, lastly, and always with the God who made them—that we should settle down here like a dove or wild eagle coming down to scratch in the barnyard with the common hens.

The reality of that other world comes to us sometimes, an invisible yet real world that is near to our world. It's a world of spirits, of God and of angels, seraphim and cherubim. Even amid our modern-day noise and confusion, there are still times, perhaps when we're alone, that we sense the other world. We know that it exists. Maybe it's only for a moment that we have such a feeling, only for a little time that it comes to us, but those times do come. We are fallen stars, made in the image of God. Fallen beings who have left their place in the celestial world and have plummeted down like stars and are here in the world, beings who have all but forgotten the place from which they came.

Occasionally, this reality comes to us in the dead of night when we're all by ourselves. Otherwise, the Devil does everything that is devilishly possible to do to prevent us from ever getting by ourselves. He uses what we glibly call the "means of communication," such as the telephone, radio, and television. The result is that we are rarely alone now. We boast that it is now possible for a person to stand on the other side of the world and speak in a well-modulated, low voice and be heard perfectly on this side of the world. Behold this great Babylon that we have created.

I think that history will probably reveal that when we invented the so-called means of communication, we made it possible for a bad singer to be heard in places on the other side of the earth instead of simply in the local place that they were mercifully confined to before, or when we make it possible for evil-minded people filled with pride to step up to a little machine and make themselves heard around the world, and we'll have to reshuffle our conclusions. In the day of Christ, I'm quite certain that our feathers will come down and we will drag along dismally instead of strutting like the bantam rooster. We'll say, "We made a great mistake."

God didn't make our voices to extend very far, a block at the most, but we've sought out many inventions and made it possible for a person's voice to circle the globe. Now we can do devilment faster and farther and bother more people, injure more nerves, harm more ears, and destroy blessed solitude more perfectly than we could in the old days when the best we could do was shout across the street.

So the Devil sees to it that we are seldom alone. But when we do manage to get alone, we sometimes sense that what we see around us isn't all there is. We say to ourselves, "I like what I see, and it has its good points, but there's something in me that tells me this isn't all there is. This just isn't it. There's something else."

You stand at the grave of a loved one to whom you have just said a tearful good-bye, and you know that this isn't it. You know there is some other world beyond the one you see. You see for a moment the invisible, and the reality of that world breaks in upon you. Most people deal with this by abruptly breaking it off and refusing to think about it at all. But one of these times, the reality of the other world will be brought vividly present before every one of us. There will be a time when a terrifying, sudden breaking off will take place. And then whether we're right or whether we're wrong, whether we're in or whether we're out of the kingdom, we'll know. There's a knowledge that's not faith anymore, a knowledge that is reality—visible, tangible, and audible. We'll know that there's another world besides the world in which we presently live.

Those who are Christians have dedicated themselves to God to inhabit another world. Isaiah saw that other world and said it was in the year King Uzziah died that he had this vision. Isaiah and Uzziah were relatives. Some say they were cousins. Isaiah was quite familiar around the court of his cousin Uzziah. Of course, with his being a relative and having entrée to the court of the king, and being a genius and a learned young man and a poet in his own right with a fine and precise mind, he must have been a very popular figure around the court. And

Uzziah was not jealous of his young friend and made a lot of him, even though Isaiah leaned hard on the king. He was an idealist.

This mighty king was dead. Isaiah stood in grief and looked down on the royal face. The royal lips didn't open to issue any decrees. The royal eyes did not stare into any of the subjects' eyes. The royal hand did not raise any scepter, and the royal head had no crown on it but lay cold and pale and quiet. All his kingly and royal parts had disappeared. He was just a dead man. Isaiah was beyond consolation.

And then Isaiah did a wise thing. He raised his eyes from looking on the dead king and fastened them instead on the living King of kings, and after that, Isaiah was a new man. He looked upon this King of kings, high and lifted up with His train filling the temple, and he had a wondrous vision.

In the kingdom of God, there's absolute freedom. I want to make that plain to you. And in God's kingdom there is no conscript angel. There is nobody who gets a summons to say that you must report at the seventh gate there in New Jerusalem, otherwise you will be considered a traitor to your country, or you'll have broken the military law or whatnot. You will not see one angel saying to another angel, "Did you get your papers yet? What's your classification?" God never, never drafts anybody. And in all of God Almighty's world—in the moral world, that is, the kingdom that is ruled by Him—there isn't one being doing anything they do not want to do. In all of God's wide domain, there isn't an angel, seraph, or archangel who is not happy to be doing what they're doing. They wouldn't do anything else if they had it offered to them. The only creatures who are otherwise are the angels who sinned and the human race. And they got themselves into their own bondage. They wanted to be free, and they became bound. Thus instead of freedom, we got bondage.

The seraphim were free, absolutely free. And that's where the holiness lies, in the fact that they could have sinned but didn't and wouldn't ever. They served God; they were truly free.

My dear friends, the will of God is freedom. The will of God is as broad as the air to the sparrow. The will of God is as big and boundless and shoreless as the ocean to the minnow. And it's only in the will of God that we find freedom. As soon as we leave the will of God, like the angels who sinned or like Satan, we come down to the level of bondage, and then we punch the clock in and out. Then we look over our shoulders and worry about the cops. Then we know that we can't do what we want to do and we're forced to do things that we don't want to do. That was what sin did to humanity.

The seventh chapter of Romans is one long groan. One long, groaning testimony of what it is not to be free, that is, if you're a man or woman who wants to do good but can't. To be someone who doesn't want to do evil and yet feels forced to do it. Sin has brought us into bondage, but in the kingdom of God, there is no bondage. There is complete freedom.

I can make the case that you cannot have morality unless you have freedom. There is a good, sound philosophy beneath the idea that you cannot have even the *idea* of morality unless you also have freedom. For just as soon as we coerce the human will, that human will can be neither good nor bad. That human will cannot do righteousness so long as it is coerced into it. And the human will that is driven to anything is not doing it freely and therefore is not doing it morally.

I think the Devil must have some bad times. I believe he forfeited his freedom when he rebelled against God. I don't want to raise any pity for him because I doubt whether he would return any pity toward us. The Devil is the Devil; he's a degraded, forsaken, and abandoned soul. I do not find anywhere in the Bible where it says God loves him or ever did love him. And I don't find anywhere where the Scripture says we're to love him.

Jesus tells us to love our enemies, but He never told us to love the Devil. He never told us to pity the Devil, yet I can't help but wonder if the Devil must not have some bad moments. He's down here with handcuffs. That's his business. He's the dispenser of handcuffs and leg-irons, and he likes to bind everybody and get them ready for hell. Then somebody breaks their chains and turns to the Lord Jesus Christ, and the Devil starts up his communistic propaganda and shouts at them, "You're being superstitious. You have gotten the chains of religion around you. You've given up the freedom of the world and have become one of those narrow Christians. You don't smoke anymore the way you used to. You don't cuss and swear the way you used to. And you don't run around and raise the devil the way you used to. You're not free anymore." Yet this just means that we don't wear the Devil's handcuffs anymore. We don't have his collar around our necks, and we don't have his leg-irons on our ankles.

One of the Devil's bad times is when he sees somebody who has served him for a great many years come to Jesus Christ. And with one quick blow, Jesus Christ breaks them free of the leg-irons and the collars and all the rest. They get down on their knees and serve God with tears and joy and kiss the holy feet of Jesus. They get up in the morning with a grateful heart and kneel to pray. Are you telling me that such a person isn't free? On the contrary, they're as free as the wide world. But they must be giving the Devil a hard time because they were told, "You're no longer free; you're in religious bondage." But the new Christian responds, "Thank God for a bondage like this. Thank God for a bondage as sweet as I find in Jesus Christ."

●　●　●　●

Our Father, we thank Thee for the example of the seraphim. I beseech Thee that we may have the same fervency that they had in their worship of the Most High. In Jesus' name, amen.

O FOR A THOUSAND TONGUES TO SING

O for a thousand tongues to sing
my great Redeemer's praise,
the glories of my God and King,
the triumphs of his grace!

My gracious Master and my God,
assist me to proclaim,
to spread through all the earth abroad
the honors of your name.

Jesus! the name that charms our fears,
that bids our sorrows cease,
'tis music in the sinner's ears,

'tis life and health and peace.

He breaks the power of canceled sin,
he sets the prisoner free;
his blood can make the foulest clean;
his blood availed for me.

Charles Wesley

16

The Power of Fire in Authentic Worship

Then Moses said, "I will now turn aside and see this great sight, why the bush does not burn."

So when the LORD saw that he turned aside to look, God called to him from the midst of the bush and said, "Moses, Moses!"

And he said, "Here I am."

Exodus 3:3–4

Moses was a great man, whose greatness was hidden and almost completely undeveloped when he encountered the burning bush. But a great career was beginning, and he was to be so many things that one wonders how God could place upon one pair of shoulders so much responsibility. He was to be a prophet under God. He was to be a lawyer. He was to be an emancipator, setting free a nation after four hundred years of slavery. He was to be the leader of the most important nation in the world, a statesman in his own right, and a teacher of the ages.

And yet Moses was not much prepared for his job. He wasn't a young man, and he couldn't go back to his youth. He just wasn't ready. However, he could have gotten on well just about anywhere, for he was educated in all the wisdom of Egypt and had been brought up within the household of the Pharaoh. The great kings of the time had dandled him on their knees when he was a little boy, and he had grown up in the courtly atmosphere of that great nation, that palace of the Pharaoh.

But after Moses had his run-in with an Egyptian, he forsook Egypt and refused to be called the son of Pharaoh's daughter. And then he took to getting himself in shape. God sent him out to keep sheep and undo some of the things his education had done for him. He sent Moses out among the smelly sheep, where he would be schooled while being surrounded by their bleating, amidst the sands and the silence and the stars.

After all of that, Moses could have been a poet, an artist, or a philosopher, but still he wasn't ready. God had to do something more for him, which He did in the encounter with the burning bush. He had to give Moses what I call a "sense of sacredness." God had to stun him, beat him down, and defeat him with this encounter. Moses had learned about theory and doctrine and was given lots of time to dream and think, but he wasn't yet ready. God could make him ready only by bringing Moses to himself through the crisis of the burning bush. He had to meet God. And so God revealed himself to the man at the bush. Alone, under the frowning brow of Sinai, Moses experienced God.

God revealed himself as fire. It's often been said that God is inscrutable and ineffable. He is a God of other things as well, but He's definitely those two things. You can't get at God with your mind. The neo-rationalism passing for Christian theology and Evangelicalism irks me because we are trying to figure out God in our heads, and it can't be done, my brethren. You can only experience God. God rises infinitely without the possibility of any man or woman grasping Him intellectually. God is ineffable, inscrutable, He cannot be spoken for, and cannot be reached. He dwells in light that no human being can approach. God presents himself through figures and similitudes, and it seems His favorite one of these is *fire*.

God came to Israel as fire. There was the fire by night and the cloud by day, and later when the tabernacle was built, the presence of God appeared as a fire between the wings of the cherubim, which they called the Shekinah. Then on the Day of Pentecost, when the Holy Ghost came upon the one hundred and twenty of the followers of Jesus gathered together, He perpetuated the idea of God as fire. He carried it over, and those disciples left with a flame of fire on their foreheads, the presence of the Almighty God. This was not some wild, irrational impulse as some people believe, but the very presence of God in the form of fire. And here God wanted to show Moses who He was by bringing Moses into an encounter with himself.

If anybody is inclined to shy away from the word *experience*, I'm not one of them. I believe in experience. Experience can be defined as a personal conscious awareness of something by someone. That someone was Moses, and the somebody he was aware of was God, and it was personal and conscious. He wasn't unconscious, and he didn't sink into his subconscious. He was awake and aware of what was going on, and his encounter with God changed him so profoundly that, afterward, he was never the same man. Moses experienced God, and from then on it was no longer theory. It was no longer knowledge just by description, but it became knowledge by experience or acquaintance.

The Scottish philosopher Thomas Carlyle (1795–1881) once walked with a minister in a garden beside a church. He linked his arm to the minister's arm and said, "Reverend, this parish needs somebody who knows God other than by hearsay." I'm convinced that many of us, even Evangelicals, know God only by hearsay. He is what we want Him to be, or hope He is, rather than what we know Him to be by spiritual encounter. And I think this is a tragic breakdown in evangelical circles, as we have used doctrine as a substitute for spiritual experience.

Spiritual experience should be the outgrowth of doctrine, but instead we make doctrine terminal. We think that if we recite the creed and understand the notes of the latest biblical commentary, we're all set. We have the knowledge, yet many people stop right there and never go on to experience God.

Bible doctrine is a highway to lead us to God, but there are many who have fallen asleep on the roadside. And because they're on the highway or near the highway, they call themselves *Evangelicals*. To me, an Evangelical is somebody not only who believes in the creeds of the Christian but who also experiences the God of the Christian. I believe there ought to be some prophets who rise in this day that live and declare that God can be experienced. We can know God. We don't have to make God a logical deduction from premises, but we can experience God as we can experience our children.

One day, my son came to meet me, along with four grandchildren, at the airport. I knew they were my grandchildren. I could prove they were by deduction, but I also knew they were my grandchildren by experience when they embraced me. And I believe as well that God can be known deep in the heart by spiritual experience.

God wanted to say some things to Moses, and He did. He defeated Moses there at the burning bush, removing all the self-confidence from the man, beating him down, and then raising him back up. This is always God's way.

There are things God taught Moses that I think He wants to teach you and me if we're going to be used at all by Him. One is that the fire dwelt in the bush, and the bush was at the mercy of the fire—that is, it accepted the rule of the fire. While it's all very well that you hold to a creed or a doctrine of God, you will never amount to anything until God holds you and uses you as an extension of His own hands. Until then, you're probably not yet where you ought to be. And this was indicated here, taught to us in a beautiful image, that the fire dwells in the bush.

I believe in the indwelling Christ; I believe in "Christ in you, the hope of glory" (Colossians 1:27). Not Christ with you only, though that's certainly true, but Christ *in* you, which is the hope of glory.

An Anglican pastor once came to me and said, "Tozer, I would like to ask you two questions. One, how do you explain the problem of the eternal God entering time? And the second one has to do with 'the true Light which gives light to every man coming into the world'" (John 1:9).

I replied, "Doctor, as for the first problem, I don't have the answer to the question. It isn't a problem to me how the eternal God can enter time below the tabernacle and become flesh to dwell among us." I waved him off, and he said, "All right. Tell me about the second one." And I did have an opinion on that, for the problem of how personality interpenetrates personality was settled for me a long time ago.

My head got ahold of it by contemplating the iron in the fire. You put the iron in the fire and blow the old-fashioned bellows until soon you have the fire in the iron. You do not have the loss of either personality. The iron is still the iron, and the fire is still the fire, but you have fused them in experience. But if the fire goes out of the iron, you still have the tool. So God enters the human breast and fuses His divine uncreated personality with His child's created personality, though they do not become metaphysically or anthropologically one. They become experientially one.

This fire, the glowing incandescence of the presence of God in the breast of the man, makes him become a little like God. There's much of God in him, yet he is not God, and God is not the man. Forever and forever, God remains God, and man remains man. Yet their personalities are united. God was trying to say this very thing to Moses, and He is saying the same to us.

Notice that the fire purified the bush. I suppose that if we were to pass around a questionnaire and ask for a definition of *sanctification* to five hundred people, they would have five hundred different definitions. For that reason, I will not get involved in doctrinal disputes over a single word. Still, I believe

God wants His people to be holy. But I do not believe holiness is ever separated from God. God is holy, and only God is holy. Where God is, there's holiness, and where God is not, there is just us. And there isn't much use in trying to make it any other way. The fire purified the bush.

Did you ever stop to think about all the fungi, bugs, larvae, worms, and everything else that perished in the bush? There wasn't a single thing there but bush and fire. I believe that the presence of God burning in the human breast purifies that breast. So long as it burns there unhindered, those evils that used to follow us around and be part of our personality will be burned away, and there will be nothing but white ash to show where they used to be.

I read that there are heatproof microbes you can boil for two hours, and they still come up smiling. They don't die. But nothing can stand raw fire, as all life dies before the flame. So, too, there are evils in the breast that can stand the presence of all kinds of revival meetings, religious meetings, and prayer meetings. And some sins can get on board and take the Lord's Supper and get baptized. But there are no sins that can stand up under the presence of the indwelling God.

It is the fire in our worship that brings it to the point of authentic worship.

*   *   *   *

O Holy Spirit, that heavenly fire from above, I praise Thee and worship Thee for all that Thou has done in my life. I am what I am today because of Your work in my life. Praise the Most High God, amen.

OLD-TIME POWER

We are gathered for Thy blessing,
We will wait upon our God;
We will trust in Him who loved us,
And who bought us with His blood.

We will glory in Thy power,
We will sing of wondrous grace;
In our midst as Thou has promised,
Come, O come and take Thy place.

Bring us low in prayer before Thee,
And with faith our souls inspire,
Till we claim, by faith, the promise
Of the Holy Ghost and fire.

Spirit, now melt and move
All of our hearts with love,
Breathe on us from above
With old-time power.

Paul Rader

17

The Beauty of God in Authentic Worship

And the Angel of the LORD appeared to him in a flame of fire
from the midst of a bush. So he looked, and behold, the bush
was burning with fire, but the bush was not consumed.

Exodus 3:2

A s we continue with Moses before the burning bush, I
want you to notice that the flame transfigured the bush.
That bush was only a scrub thornbush, and there were millions
of them growing around there.

Moses had probably seen them by the hundreds. But this
bush suddenly became the most famous bush in all of history
and remains the most famous bush to this day. Its glory was a
derived glory. God did not make the bush great; He simply got

in the bush and was great in the bush. And so the attention of everybody was called to the bush.

Regardless of one's level of curiosity, all of us would likely have felt compelled to turn to see a fire in a bush at sundown miles from human habitation, and that was all Moses did. He turned aside to see the transfigured bush. It took on meaning and significance. It was related by nature to all the other acacia bushes, yet nobody ever talked about them. They all talk about that one bush. Why? Because it had the fire in it. One of the saddest things I know is the anonymity of the average man. Emerson said the average man and woman is only one more couple.

Go out on the highways or down on the street corners or into the far jungle areas wherever you will—east or west, north or south—and you will find thousands of people crawling like animated clothespins over the face of the earth. They're born, they live, suffer, and have a bit of joy. Then they die, and the world knows them no more. They're faceless, without significance and meaning. But when Jesus Christ lays hold of a person, the first thing He does is to give them significance. They amount to something. God gives them a face and dwells in them, and they become transfigured in the fire. And the faceless ones touched by the mighty Christ now take on significance and meaning. They've taken on a meaning they never had before, and nobody can have it except by the fire.

No evil could bother that bush as long as the fire was in it. A hungry rabbit browsing at twilight wouldn't have gone near that bush. No, the rabbit would go to another one. Same goes for the buzzard looking around; he wouldn't venture near the bush. Nor a bug or a caterpillar that would crawl up on it. The bush was perfectly safe as long as the fire dwelt in it.

I believe in separation, but I don't believe in insulation. And I don't believe it's the will of God that His evangelical believers, His children, should insulate themselves from others. If you're reluctant to associate with others, how can you speak to them about the Lord? Suppose we are to draw our holy skirts about us, wrap ourselves in cellophane, mark heaven on us, and expect to get there when finally we pass through customs. I wonder how we could help anybody all insulated like that.

We are to be separated, but we are certainly not blessed just to be wrapped in cellophane. Monasticism, historically, was Christians saying, "I've got my fire, and now I'm going to have to cup it and keep it." So they cupped their hands around it so the wind wouldn't blow it out, and they went to the monasteries. This was a mistake. I honor them for their intention, but it doesn't speak too much about their knowledge of the Scriptures.

Simeon Stylites was probably the most notorious example of an effort to be good by getting away from people. He climbed up onto a pillar thirty feet high and stayed there for thirty-seven years. He never came down, even to take a bath. In fact, he never came down for anything. So they sent up his food, which he would pull up the pillar using a rope. And in this way he thought he was being holy. But the Son of God walked among the people, among publicans and sinners, and talked at the well to a fallen woman. He was holy and pure because the purity was inside Him.

We do, in truth, become pure. We do not become safe by hiding. Instead, we become safe by the indwelling fire. I'm perfectly convinced that nothing can harm that human breast when God dwells in it. Nothing can harm that individual until God wants the person in heaven with Him.

Maybe this is the most important thing for us in our work as believers. The bush became beautiful in the fire. Moses, many years later, wrote, "Let the beauty of the LORD our God be upon us" (Psalm 90:17). I wonder if Moses was thinking of the beauty of God in the bush, that solemn, wonderful hour when he saw God and met Him in the fire: "Let the beauty of the LORD our God be upon us."

Though the ancient Greek philosophers had no revelation to speak of, sometimes they stumbled upon the truth. They believed that beauty was somehow near to God. And here was a bush that nobody would have brought home and planted in their yard. It had no beauty to speak of. Yet now this one was beautiful because it was aglow.

St. Bernard of Clairvaux beseeches in his poem, "Stay, O Beauty uncreated, ever ancient, ever new. . . ." When Jesus came down to become man, His garments smelled of myrrh and aloes and cashew out of the ivory palaces. We pass through hectic Christmas seasons, but if you can get past the lights and Santa Claus and the rest of it, you will see the beauty of Jesus and smell the fragrance of the myrrh, aloes, and cashew from His holy garments. Though He was sleeping on a hill outside of Jerusalem, the fragrance of His life made the world smell much better. This dirty world is beautiful because He was here.

There's an attractiveness to true Christianity. I don't mind confessing that I'm not as happy a man as I ought to be, and one of the things I am miserable about is the unattractiveness of Christianity in our day. Unattractive or unlovely Christianity is without a doubt one of the major tragedies today.

But how do we start?

I believe in saints. I've met the comics, I've met the promoters, and I've met the founders who put their names on the fronts of buildings so that people know who founded them. I've met converted cowboys who are not too well converted, and I've met converted pugilists who are converted everywhere but in their fists. I've met all kinds of strange Christians throughout the United States and Canada, but my heart is looking for saints. I want to meet people like the Lord Jesus Christ.

My brothers and sisters, you're called to be a burning bush, a bush with fire in it. This is the world's sundown. And there are men like Moses, alone and searching for somebody who looks like God, somebody who has fire in them. Lonely people everywhere are looking in your direction. And it's my conviction that unlovely Christianity has done more to turn more people away from Christ than all the liberalism in the world.

I'm not a liberal; I'm an Evangelical and an essentialist—a believer in historic Christianity and the faith of our fathers, which is living still. And yet I believe that until evangelical Christianity meets God in the fire and gets God burning and glowing within it, we're going to have all these troubles, and we're not going to solve them by attending conferences.

We're not going to solve this basic problem of unattractive Christianity unless we solve it on our knees. It's not a technique or a method to be followed. It's the individual person and their God. God and the individual. Each of us in God, and God in each of us—the fire, the Holy Ghost, burning in the breast of each Christian. Brothers and sisters, if the fire burns hot enough, it will burn through an awful lot of problems that you won't be able to solve in a panel discussion of a thousand people. May God help us as we go out to serve Him in His world. May we remember that the most important thing is that we should meet God himself in a living, vivid spiritual encounter.

*   *   *   *

Blessed Father, we pray that Thou will take these words and plant them deep in our hearts. We pray for a great longing after Thee. We pray for an overwhelming desire to have a living encounter through the Holy Spirit until all our self-confidence is gone and we rest in our God alone. We ask these things in Jesus' name, amen.

LIVING IN THE GLORY

I have found a heav'n below,
I am living in the glory;
O! the joy and strength I know,
Living in the glory of the Lord.

Storms of sorrow 'round me fall,
But I'm living in the glory;
I can sing above them all,
Living in the glory of the Lord.

I can triumph over pain
While I'm living in the glory;
I can count each loss a gain,
Living in the glory of the Lord.

Soon the King will come for me,
To be with Him in the glory;

Then my sweeter song shall be
Reigning in the glory of the Lord.

Yes, I'm living in the glory,
As He promised in His word;
I am dwelling in the heav'nlies,
Living in the glory of the Lord.

Albert B. Simpson

18

Conclusion

I hope that the message in this book has been clearly understood. This is just the beginning of what worship is all about. We can go on and on forever and not cover the entirety of the subject.

But I've covered what is important to me about this matter of authentic worship. The more I know, the more I understand I don't know, but the great thing is that my fascination for worship drives me to worship.

I realize this is a book on worship, and yet learning *how* to worship doesn't come from a book. A book may inspire you to do something, but then it's up to you to put it into practice. We have all these things before us, but still we often get caught up with the mundane things of the world so that we lose our interest in what is so critical, and that is worship.

Over the years, I've noticed how worship has grown and expanded. When I was first converted, I was very much interested in worship and did everything I could to follow through on my desire to learn more. As I grew older, my idea and understanding of worship grew as well. My worship back then was not so much like how I worship now. Should I live another fifty years, my prayer is that my worship then will be much greater that it is now.

My worship should separate me from the world but not from other believers. This can be a hard thing to do. It's easy to get all caught up in personal worship, and I'm all for that and I practice that. But it's another thing to gather as brothers and sisters in the Lord and worship Him together. That is the genius of the New Testament church.

Church is not for social events or feeding the hungry or raising money for missions. All of these might be right things to do, and I'm not against them at all, but I think the Church's main responsibility is to create an environment for worship. And that worship needs to be separated from the world.

I have noticed lately that much of the music style of the world is coming into the Church. I've also noticed that not many churches are singing hymns. How can you be a New Testament church and not glorify God by singing a hymn? I know many are saying that this is old-fashioned and we need to be up to date. Personally, I don't want to be up to date with the world. I don't want to be in tune with the world.

I don't think worship at church should in any way attract the world. If it does, something is wrong. To try to use Sunday morning as an evangelistic meeting is to misunderstand what Sunday worship is all about.

If you go back to the early church in the book of Acts, you will find that the world separated themselves from the church. They do not want anything do with the church.

I think if we would have New Testament churches today that are biblically oriented and exercise authentic worship as I outlined in this book, we will see a great change in the Church at large today. This is a change that really needs to come.

I've said this before, and I want to repeat it here: If, when I go to work on Monday morning, I'm not as enthusiastic or passionate about worshiping God as I was the day before, maybe what I did the day before wasn't really worship. Another thing I want to stress is this: If my worship doesn't cost me anything, it's not genuine. It's not authentic worship as I have presented it in this book.

It would be a terrible thing if after many years of thinking I was a Christian, I died and stood before God and He said, "I never knew you; depart from Me, you who practice lawlessness!" (Matthew 7:23). After all those years of thinking I was doing the right thing and serving the Lord, only to find out it was not authentic? No, I don't want to have lived my whole life in a false cloud.

A final thing I need to state is that I do not take credit for your passion for worship. I'm simply encouraging you, and the rest of it is up to you. Your passion for worship must come from deep inside of you. It must be a passion that nobody can siphon.

When I die, I look forward to standing in front of the Lord Jesus Christ and Him saying with a smile on His face, "Well done, good and faithful servant. Enter into the joy of your Lord" (Matthew 25:23). Nothing else really matters.

Everything I do is based on the fact that I want to be a faithful servant, and I want to explore as much as possible the authentic worship of the Most High God.

WHEN MORNING GILDS THE SKIES

When morning gilds the skies,
My heart awaking cries:
May Jesus Christ be praised!
Alike at work and prayer,
To Jesus I repair:
May Jesus Christ be praised!

Does sadness fill my mind?
A solace here I find,
May Jesus Christ be praised!
Or fades my earthly bliss?
My comfort still is this,
May Jesus Christ be praised!

The night becomes as day
When from the heart we say:
May Jesus Christ be praised!
The powers of darkness fear
When this sweet chant they hear:
May Jesus Christ be praised!

Edward Caswall

A.W. Tozer (1897–1963) was a self-taught theologian, pastor, and writer whose powerful words continue to grip the intellect and stir the soul of today's believer. He authored more than forty books. *The Pursuit of God* and *The Knowledge of the Holy* are considered modern devotional classics. Get Tozer information and quotes at twitter.com/TozerAW.

Reverend James L. Snyder is an award-winning author whose writings have appeared in more than eighty periodicals and fifteen books. He is recognized as an authority on the life and ministry of A.W. Tozer. His first book, *The Life of A.W. Tozer: In Pursuit of God*, won the Readers' Choice Award in 1992 by *Christianity Today*. Because of his thorough knowledge of Tozer, James was given the rights from the A.W. Tozer estate to produce new books derived from over four hundred never-before-published audiotapes. James and his wife live in Ocala, Florida. Learn more at awtozerclassics.com, or contact James at jamessnyder51@gmail.com.

More from A.W. Tozer

Not knowing *how to pray* is one of the greatest obstacles in a Christian's life. In *Going Higher with God in Prayer*, Tozer challenges you to ask: Are my prayers more powerful and effective today than they were a year ago? Only God can teach us what is on His heart, what is His will, and what our part in it can be.

Going Higher with God in Prayer

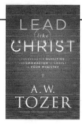

As a Christian, does your leadership approach look any different from that of those who don't follow Christ? Rather than focusing on the nuts and bolts of management, *Lead like Christ* looks closely at how leaders can imitate the greatest Leader of all. This step of humility and obedience will result in powerful, long-lasting change in your leadership role.

Lead like Christ

More than 70 years after its original release, this A.W. Tozer classic continues to resonate in the heart of anyone longing for a deeper experience with God. Now available in an appealing hardcover gift edition, this book invites you to think deeply about your faith and will lead you to the only One who can satisfy your soul.

The Pursuit of God